REVISE AQA GCSE (9–1) German
REVISION WORKBOOK

Series Consultant: Harry Smith

Author: Harriette Lanzer

Also available to support your revision:

Revise GCSE Study Skills Guide 9781447967071

The **Revise GCSE Study Skills Guide** is full of tried-and-trusted hints and tips for how to learn more effectively. It gives you techniques to help you achieve your best – throughout your GCSE studies and beyond!

Revise GCSE Revision Planner 9781447967828

The **Revise GCSE Revision Planner** helps you to plan and organise your time, step-by-step, throughout your GCSE revision. Use this book and wall chart to mastermind your revision.

Difficulty scale

The scale next to each exam-style question tells you how difficult it is.

Some questions cover a range of difficulties.

The more of the scale that is shaded, the harder the question is.

 Some questions are Foundation level.

 Some questions are Higher level.

 Some questions are applicable to both levels.

For the full range of Pearson revision titles across KS2, KS3, GCSE, Functional Skills, AS/A Level and BTEC visit:
www.pearsonschools.co.uk/revise

Contents

AUDIO

Audio files and transcripts for the listening exercises in this book can be accessed by using the QR codes throughout the book, or going to **www.pearsonschools.co.uk/ mflrevisionaudio**

Listen to the recording

A small bit of small print

AQA publishes Sample Assessment Material and the Specification on its website. This is the official content and this book should be used in conjunction with it. The questions in this Workbook have been written to help you practise every topic in the book. Remember: the real exam questions may not look like this.

Physical descriptions

Personal profiles

1   Read the personal profiles on a dating website.

Write the first letter of the correct name in the box.

Write **M** for **Michael**.
Write **N** for **Nils**.
Write **R** for **Robert**.
Write **A** for **Albert**.

● ● ●	
MICHAEL H.	Ich bin gr**öß**er als meine Freunde und auch sehr schlank. Ich habe braune, glatte Haare – sie sehen oft ein bisschen wild aus!
NILS D.	Meine Augen sind grün und ich trage immer eine Brille. Ich habe einen langen Bart.
ROBERT W.	Ich trage gern einen großen Ohrring im linken Ohr, weil ich das cool finde, aber ich habe keinen Schnurrbart – ich finde das hässlich!
ALBERT F.	Ich habe eine Glatze, also muss ich nie zum Friseur gehen. Ich bin froh darüber!

> Don't be confused by a comparative such as *größer* from *groß*, just because it has an umlaut.

(a) Who wears jewellery?   R   **(1 mark)**

(b) Who does not have perfect eyesight?   N   **(1 mark)**

(c) Who often looks untidy?   M   **(1 mark)**

(d) Who does not have any hair?   A   **(1 mark)**

(e) Who has facial hair?   R   **(1 mark)**

Missing child

2   Frau Richter is describing her missing child, Annabell, at the police station in Germany.

Which statement is true?

Write the correct letter in the box.

(a)

A	Annabell has curly hair.
B	Annabell wears glasses.
C	Annabell is wearing a T-shirt.

☐   **(1 mark)**

(b)

A	Annabell often goes out on her own.
B	Annabell has an umbrella with her.
C	Annabell does not have a mobile.

☐   **(1 mark)**

Character descriptions

Family blog

1 You read Sura's blog on an Austrian family website.

> ● ○ ○
>
> Heute schreibe ich über meinen jüngeren Bruder Kadir. Er ist fünfzehn Jahre alt und wir verstehen uns seit der Kindheit wirklich sehr gut, weil wir viele Interessen gemeinsam haben. Als Kadir sehr klein war, war er schüchtern und ziemlich ernst. Wenn ein Erwachsener ihm eine Frage stellte, musste ich als seine ältere Schwester die Antwort darauf geben.
>
> Jetzt braucht Kadir mich nicht mehr so sehr, weil er viel selbstbewusster ist. Sogar mit älteren Leuten ist er offen und freundlich und er kommt allen gar nicht zurückhaltend vor. Ich bin zwar ein bisschen faul, aber Kadir ist das nie, weil er zu viel Energie hat, um bloß auf dem Sofa zu sitzen! In der Schule ist er besonders fleißig und er hat nie Probleme mit den Hausaufgaben, obwohl ich finde, dass er zu oft Informationen direkt vom Internet abschreibt.
>
> Kadir ist drei Jahre jünger als ich und wir haben beide unsere eigenen Freundeskreise, aber wenn wir zu Hause sind, findet Kadir immer Zeit für mich.
>
> **Sura**

Read the text first of all for the gist. Then read it again, keeping an eye on the statements you have to choose from.

According to Sura, which of the following **four** statements are true?

A	Sura has an older brother, Kadir.
B	Sura and Kadir have always had the same interests.
C	Kadir dislikes the activities his sister, Sura, enjoys.
D	Kadir used to be more confident than Sura.
E	Sura used to answer questions for Kadir.
F	Kadir finds it hard to talk to adults now.
G	Kadir never lazes about at home.
H	Kadir finds time to be with his sister.

Write the correct letters in the boxes.

☐ ☐ ☐ ☐

(4 marks)

Neighbours

2 You are talking to some Swiss teenagers about their neighbours.

Write **in English** each person's opinion of their neighbour and the reason for it.

Listen to the recording

(a)

Opinion	
Reason	

(1 mark)

(1 mark)

(b)

Opinion	
Reason	

(1 mark)

(1 mark)

2

Childhood

> The General Conversation is the final section in the Speaking exam. It should last 3–5 minutes for Foundation and 5–7 minutes for Higher. You need to ask your teacher a question during the conversation.

Matching questions and answers

1 Match the student replies (A–E) to the teacher's questions (1–5). Draw lines to link them.

1 Woran erinnerst du dich am meisten aus deiner Kindheit?

> Have a good supply of idioms and expressions which you can transfer to any topic, such as *meiner Meinung nach* and *es ist schade, dass …*

A Mit fünf Jahren ist man meiner Meinung nach viel zu jung, um in die Schule zu gehen. In Deutschland ist es besser, weil man erst mit sechs Jahren in die Schule muss. Es ist schade, dass wir das hier in England nicht machen.

2 Was hast du gern in der Grundschule gemacht?

B Ich erinnere mich besonders an den Kindergarten, denn wir haben den ganzen Tag nur gebastelt und gespielt. Das hat echt viel Spaß gemacht.

3 In welchem Alter sollte man mit der Schule anfangen?

C Ich würde ein Schwimmbad an der Schule bauen, damit die Kinder schwimmen lernen und dann richtig im Meer und im Freibad schwimmen können. Außerdem würde ich den Stundenplan mit interessanteren Fächern füllen.

4 Wie werden Kinder in der Zukunft anders leben?

D In der Grundschule war ich ziemlich schüchtern und ich habe oft alleine auf dem Pausenhof gespielt. Ich habe die Fächer nicht so interessant gefunden, aber die Grundschullehrer waren sehr sympathisch.

5 Wie würdest du deine frühere Grundschule verbessern?

E Kinder werden in ein paar Jahren immer noch genauso sein wie jetzt. Sie werden immer noch mit Puppen und Fußbällen spielen und sie werden immer noch weinen und lachen. Bestimmt werden sie öfter am Bildschirm sitzen und daher werden sie nicht sehr gesund sein.

2 Listen to the student's answers, paying particular attention to the pronunciation of words with umlauts such as *Fächern*, *fünf* and *öfter*.

Listen to the recording

3

Family

My family

1   You read Till's blog on a family website.

Answer the questions **in English**.

> ● ● ●
>
> Obwohl ich Einzelkind bin, habe ich mich nie einsam gefühlt. Als ich in der Grundschule war, haben wir in Frankfurt gewohnt. In derselben Stadt waren meine Großeltern und meine Tanten, und es hat mir viel Spaß gemacht, einmal pro Woche mit meinen zwei Cousinen zu spielen.
>
> Weil meine Eltern oft bis zehn Uhr abends arbeiten mussten, hat meine Tante Julia nach der Schule auf mich aufgepasst. Meine Tante ist ebenso streng wie Mutti und Vati, und ich musste immer Hausaufgaben machen, bevor ich spielen oder fernsehen durfte.
>
> Vor vier Jahren mussten wir nach Bonn ziehen, weil meine Eltern sich dort erfolgreich auf Stellen bei einer großen Firma beworben haben. Ich bin sehr traurig, dass ich meine Umgebung sowie meine Cousinen verlassen musste und jetzt weit von ihnen entfernt wohne.

(a)   How many brothers and sisters does Till have? a an onlychild   **(1 mark)**

(b)   Name **one** adult family member who helped look after Till during his childhood.

his aunt Julia   **(1 mark)**

(c)   Why did Till need help after school? his parent work alot   **(1 mark)**

(d)   What did Till think of his aunt? she is strict   **(1 mark)**

(e)   Why is Till now living in Bonn? parents new firm(job)   **(1 mark)**

(f)   How does Till feel about his current situation?

Write the correct letter in the box.

A	happy
B	sad
C	relieved

C   **(1 mark)**

> You do not have to write complete sentences for comprehension questions, either in English or in German, but you do need to answer the question you are asked and in the language you are asked to reply in – make sure you read the question words carefully.

Familien in Not

2   Du sprichst mit Frau Hartfiel von einem Wohltätigkeitsverein für Familien.

Beantworte alle Teile der Frage **auf Deutsch**.

Listen to the recording

(a)   Warum ist es überraschend, dass manche Familien in Österreich in Not sind?

....   **(1 mark)**

(b)   Was für Probleme haben manche Schüler?

....

....   **(2 marks)**

(c)   Welche Familien haben öfters solche Probleme?

....   **(1 mark)**

Friends

My friends

1   Translate the following sentences **into German**.

> You will not be allowed a dictionary in the exam, but while you are revising it can help to use one to remind yourself of vocabulary.

(a)   I love my friends.

Guided

Ich liebe .....meine Freunde.........................

(b)   My friend Lottie is very nice.

Meine ....Freundin Lottie ist sehr...........

nett..

> Revise possessive adjectives, such as *mein*, *dein* and *unser*, and their endings – look at page 88 in the Grammar section to check.

(c)   She lives next to a station in Berlin.

Sie wohnt in Berlin netzts das Station.................

....

(d)   We often go to the cinema together.

Wir fahren oft in kino together........................

....

(e)   Last time we laughed a lot.

Letztes viel, haben wir viele.......................

laughed..

> You will need to translate sentences about other people and not just the *ich* form – look at page 91 in the Grammar section to check your pronouns.

....

(10 marks)

My friends

2   Translate the following passage **into German**.

> I often play computer games with my friend, Tom. Yesterday I was at his house but his brother <u>was</u> very <u>annoying</u>. Tom <u>will</u> come to my house <u>tomorrow</u>. I find it better when he comes on his <u>own</u>, because that is <u>much</u> more fun.

> There are 12 marks for this task and four sentences to be translated, which become progressively more difficult. Divide up the time available to make sure you translate each sentence.

Guided

Ich ...spiele oft mit mein Freund Tom Computerspiele.

....

Gestern ,,war ich zum ihre Hause aber ihre Bruder

wort sehr anstrengend.

Tom ..wird hier nach meine

Hause kommen. Ich finde

es besser wann er kommt

auf ihre own, denn dass

ist much mehr Spaß.

> Conjunctions such as *aber* do not affect the word order.

> Remember the word order: Time (tomorrow), Manner, Place (house) – make sure you follow this here.

> Make sure you are confident with the different tenses – present, past, future and the conditional form could all come up. See page 103 in the Grammar section for the future tense to use here.

(12 marks)

Peer group

Friendship groups

1   Look at the photo and read the task.

> Du machst einen Ausflug mit deinen Freunden und schickst dieses Foto an deinen Freund in Österreich.
>
> Schreib **vier** Sätze **auf Deutsch** über das Foto.

Now combine the sentence halves to read this student's response to the activity.

> Using conjunctions such as *weil* and *dass* shows good command of the German language with the verb sent to the end of the clause.

1   Ich bin mit

2   Mein bester Freund trägt

3   Wir <u>treffen uns</u> nach der Schule <u>hier</u>, weil

4   Der Park ist schön,

(a)   aber manchmal gibt es <u>dort Abfall.</u>

(b)   wir in der Nähe wohnen.

(c)   meinen Freunden am Skateboardpark.

(d)   eine kurze Hose und ein weißes T-Shirt.

My photo message

2   Now complete the activity yourself.

> Make sure you write four separate sentences – each one describing something you can see in the photo.

Drei Personnen in dem Foto sind glücklich.

(2 marks)

Sie sind am Skateboardparu.

(2 marks)

Das Wetter ist schön aber ziemlich windig

In der Hinde kumft,

(2 marks)

Auf die rechts, er hat ein Skateboard <u>vor ihr</u>

(2 marks)

6

Marriage

Translation

1 Translate this description **into English**.

> Meine Tante heiratet ihren Partner. Ihr neuer Mann ist sehr lustig und nett. Er ist sechsundvierzig Jahre alt und arbeitet in einem Büro. Wir <u>feiern</u> <u>zuerst</u> in der Kirche und dann in einem Restaurant. Am Wochenende habe ich ein neues Kleid gekauft.

> When you translate a passage into English, don't make careless errors such as forgetting to translate a word or translating a sentence into a different tense from the original.

Guided

My aunt is married to her partner. He new husband

Her new husband is very funny and nice.

> Check page 88 in the Grammar section to make sure that you know your possessive adjectives, especially *ihr* (her) and *sein* (his).

He is 46 years old and works in a bank.

We firstly go out to the Kirche and then in a Restaurant.

> Watch out for the past tense sentence at the end of this passage and translate it accurately.

At the weekend I bought a new shirt

(9 marks)

Wedding planner

2 While listening to German radio, you hear a wedding planner, Herr Kreitling, talking about the service he offers.

Write the correct letters in the boxes.

(a) Wedding planners are …

A	growing in popularity.
B	unfashionable.
C	very expensive.

☐

(1 mark)

(b) Most couples don't have the … to plan their wedding party.

A	desire
B	skill
C	time

☐

(1 mark)

(c) A wedding planner …

A	is expensive but useful.
B	alleviates stress.
C	is only for a few people.

☐

(1 mark)

(d) Wedding celebrations have to be …

A	unique.
B	local.
C	expensive.

☐

(1 mark)

Partnerships

Die Partnersuche

1 Lies diesen Artikel über die Partnersuche.

Beantworte die Fragen **auf Deutsch**.

> Ein junger Mann sitzt im Wohnzimmer und tippt auf der Tastatur seines Computers. Er hofft, dass eine neue Nachricht von einer zukünftigen Partnerin auf ihn wartet und er geht direkt zur Partnervermittlungs-Webseite ‚Liebe für alle'.
>
> Sein Profil sieht noch gut aus, denkt er, als er das Foto vom letzten Urlaub in Griechenland lächelnd anblickt. „Das war eine tolle Reise", meint er, „ich habe eine Menge nette Leute kennengelernt, aber leider wohnen sie alle weit weg. So geht das bei Urlaubsbekanntschaften."
>
> Der junge Mann benutzt – wie viele seiner Generation – Online-Dating-Seiten, um die ideale Partnerin zu treffen. Aber wird er erfolgreich sein?

> You need to be familiar with the German question words here – check page 106 in the Grammar section to make sure you know the main ones.

(a) Wo ist der junge Mann?

Guided im .... **(1 mark)**

(b) Was gefällt ihm auf der Webseite?

.... **(1 mark)**

(c) Wer war mit diesem Mann auch im Urlaub?

.... **(1 mark)**

(d) Laut dem Artikel, wird der Mann Erfolg in der Liebe haben?

.... **(1 mark)**

Opinions on partnerships

2 You are listening to a TV debate about people's opinions on civil partnerships in Germany.

What is their opinion on the topic?

Write **P** for a **positive** opinion.

Listen to the recording

Write **N** for a **negative** opinion.

Write **P + N** for a **positive and a negative** opinion.

> Listen to the entire extract before deciding what to write in the box – if the speaker offers a new and opposite opinion at the end, that will change your answer.

(a) Angela

[   ] **(1 mark)**

(b) Peter

[   ] **(1 mark)**

(c) Corinna

[   ] **(1 mark)**

(d) Tobias

[   ] **(1 mark)**

Social media

Swiss teenagers and social media

Listen to the recording

1   While on holiday in Switzerland, you hear an expert discussing the topic of social media and teenagers on the radio.

Answer all the questions **in English.**

Part (a)

(i)   What percentage of young people have a social media profile?

.... **(1 mark)**

(ii)   What **two** things do the networks facilitate?

....

.... **(2 marks)**

(iii)   Why is it easy for some people to abuse social networks?

.... **(1 mark)**

> Underline key words in the questions before you listen, to help you focus on the answers.

Part (b)

Now listen to a teenage contributor to the radio programme and answer these questions **in English.**

(i)   What does this young person find particularly positive about social media?

> Watch out – if there are separable verbs in listening extracts, you might not hear the whole verb until the end of the clause.

.... **(1 mark)**

(ii)   How did he overcome a problem in the past?

.... **(1 mark)**

(iii)   What **two** reasons does he give for why adults store up trouble for themselves?

....

.... **(2 marks)**

Mobile technology

My technology

1 Three Swiss teenagers have written blogs about their use of technology.

Read their blogs and complete the sentences **in English**.

Liam

Ich simse jeden Tag, denn ich finde das sehr praktisch. Ich sehe manchmal einen spannenden Film auf einem Tablet, obwohl das auf dem großen Bildschirm im Kino besser ist. Ich lade nie Lieder herunter, weil ich mich nicht sehr für Musik interessiere.

(a) Every day, Liam ....   **(1 mark)**

(b) Liam watches films on a tablet, even though ....   **(1 mark)**

(c) Liam never ....   **(1 mark)**

Mia

Meine Freunde benutzen immer ihre Handys zu Hause, aber meine Familie ist streng dagegen, und Handys sind bei uns am Tisch verboten. Während der Woche benutze ich aber oft mein Handy, weil ich gern mit meinen Freundinnen aufregende Pläne mache. Im Moment spart mein Bruder auf einen neuen Computer, weil er gern die neuesten Videospiele spielt.

(d) Mia's family is ....   **(1 mark)**

(e) Mia likes ....   **(1 mark)**

(f) Mia's brother likes ....   **(1 mark)**

Jakob

Ich benutze meistens Technologie, um schnelle Einkäufe online zu machen. Auch wenn ich Zeit habe, will ich absolut nicht ins Einkaufszentrum gehen, weil das langweilig ist.

(g) Jakob uses technology to ....   **(1 mark)**

(h) Even if Jakob has the time, he does not ....   **(1 mark)**

> Build a word bank for yourself, starting with the adjectives on this page, and add to them as you work through the book – they will stand you in good stead across all four skills in the exams.

Online activities

Topic: Technology in everyday life

My photo description

1   Look at the picture-based task for the photo and read this student's answers to the first two bullet points. Then prepare your own answers to the remaining three bullet points.

Guided

• **Was gibt es auf dem Foto?**

Das Bild zeigt ein Mädchen, das auf seinem Bett liegt. Sie ist ein Teenager und sie hat lange, glatte Haare. Sie trägt Kopfhörer und sie lächelt, weil sie glücklich ist. Im Vordergrund hat sie einen Computer, aber sie benutzt ihn nicht, weil sie sich auf das Handy konzentriert. Das Mädchen trägt einen hellen, kurzen Pullover und ihr Schlafzimmer sieht schön aus.

> Your first task is to say something factual about the photo, i.e. **describe** what you can see. You could describe where it is set, who is in it, what they are wearing, or anything else you can **see** in the photo.

> This student has used a relative pronoun here (*ein Mädchen, das*) – a useful construction to use when describing a person in a picture.

• **Wie findest du Online-Aktivitäten und warum?**

Ich finde Online-Aktivitäten super, weil sie so praktisch sind. Wenn ich Probleme mit den Hausaufgaben habe, suche ich die Informationen sofort im Internet. Es ist auch gut, dass man Kinokarten online kaufen kann, weil das Zeit spart. Schlecht daran ist aber, dass man vielleicht zu viel Zeit am Bildschirm verbringt. Es ist sicher gefährlich, wenn man stundenlang am Computer sitzt.

> Here you need to give your opinion. Words such as *Meinung, meinen, denken, finden* all indicate your teacher is looking for an opinion. You can use the present tense for this.

• **Was hast du gestern online gemacht?**
• **! (Was willst du heute Abend online machen?)**
• **! (Meinst du, Technologie ist unterhaltsam und lustig?)**

> These are your two unprepared questions on the photo. The first one refers to the future with a modal construction. Make sure you use this in your answer: *Heute Abend will ich … machen.*

> Your second unprepared question is looking for your opinion. Start with a phrase such as: *Ich finde, Ich glaube, Meiner Meinung nach ist …*

2   Look at the Answers section on page 122 to read and listen to the student's answers to all five bullet points.

> If you don't say enough in response to a bullet point, your teacher may prompt you with further questions, such as: *Warum? Warum nicht? Noch etwas?*

> Practise your pronunciation – listen to the first response and repeat it after the speaker. Record yourself so you can listen to how 'German' you sound. Key sounds to get right here include: *Mädchen, hübsch, Vordergrund, weil, sich, schön.*

For and against technology

Translation

1 Translate this description **into English**.

> Ich bin täglich online und lade gern Fotos hoch. Der größte Vorteil für mich ist, dass ich mit Freunden immer in Kontakt stehe. Auf der anderen Seite würde ich nie wieder Einkäufe online machen. Letztes Jahr ist mir das Risiko des virtuellen Lebens klar geworden, als jemand meine persönlichen Daten gestohlen hat.

Guided

I am ....
....
....
The biggest ....
....
....
On the other ....
....
....
Last ....
....
....

> Use word associations and context to help you understand unfamiliar words: if you don't know what *täglich* means, think about the word *Tag* and also the context here in the present tense, to see if they bring you closer to the word you are looking for.

> Similarities with other words you do know can sometimes be more obscure: *Einkäufe* may throw you, if you don't see the link with the familiar verb *einkaufen* (to shop).

(9 marks)

Technology pros and cons

2 Your German teacher is talking about her students and technology.

Answer the questions **in English**.

(a) How often does Benn use social networks?

Write the correct letter in the box.

Listen to the recording

A	Every day
B	Once a week
C	Never

☐

> Don't jump to the conclusion that **A** must be correct as soon as you hear the word *jeden*. Read what the question is asking, not just the answer options.

(1 mark)

(b) What is Timo unable to do at the moment?

....

(1 mark)

Everyday life

Adverts

1 While on holiday in Austria, you hear this advert on the radio.

Choose the correct answer to complete each sentence.

Write the correct letters in the boxes.

> Listen to the recording first to get the gist of the advert. Then concentrate on the multiple choice options and see how many you can identify, and also if there are any answer options you can discount straight away.

(a) This advert claims the tea will help people to …

A	sleep better.
B	do athletics.
C	get out of bed.

☐

> You might hear all these answer options in the recording, but it is the one thing which the tea will help people with that is key here.

(1 mark)

(b) The advert is aimed at …

A	single people.
B	people with families.
C	schools.

☐

> Make sure you don't switch off during listening activities – the recording will keep going, even if you don't!

(1 mark)

2 Now listen to another advert and write the correct letters in the boxes.

(a) This advert claims that …

A	most work days vary.
B	every work day is the same.
C	routines are positive.

☐

(1 mark)

(b) The advert is aimed at …

A	people who love their jobs.
B	people who find their jobs dull.
C	homeless people.

☐

> During your second listening, make sure you do not leave any answer boxes blank – you will not hear the recording again, so you must be definite with your decision-making here.

(1 mark)

Hobbies

Website profile

1 Marven has sent you a link to his homepage.

> Ich bin musikalisch und spiele gern Klavier. Ich übe dreimal pro Woche und am Samstagnachmittag habe ich eine Stunde Unterricht.
>
> Ich lerne auch Schlagzeug, aber das spiele ich nicht im Schlafzimmer. Das muss ich in der Garage spielen.
>
> Ich höre auch gern Musik. Früher habe ich gern Popmusik und Volksmusik gehört, aber jetzt finde ich die total schrecklich. Rockmusik und Tanzmusik finde ich besonders toll, und auch klassische Musik.

Answer the questions **in English**.

(a) What instrument does Marven practise three times a week?

.... **(1 mark)**

(b) Where does he play the drums?

.... **(1 mark)**

(c) Give **two** types of music Marven likes listening to.

....

....

.... **(2 marks)**

> Watch out for question (c)! You need types of music Marven **likes** listening to, not just a type of music he mentions.

Kai's hobbies

Listen to the recording

2 Your exchange partner, Kai, has sent you a podcast about his hobbies.

(a) What **two** negative aspects of his winter hobby does he mention?

Complete the table **in English**.

> You have to keep up with the recording – it will not stop to allow you time to catch up in the exam.

	Aspect 1	**Aspect 2**
Negative		

(2 marks)

(b) What **two** positive aspects of his summer hobby does he mention?

Complete the table **in English**.

	Aspect 1	**Aspect 2**
Positive		

(2 marks)

Interests

Jugendinteressen

1   Du liest in der Schweiz diesen Artikel über einen Treffpunkt zum Thema Jugend: Hobbys, Sport, Musik, Mode ... und viel, viel mehr.

Beantworte die Fragen **auf Deutsch**. Vollständige Sätze sind nicht nötig.

● ● ●

„Wer kommt tanzen?", „Spielen wir heute Fußball?", „Stellt die Musik lauter!", „Freitagabend ist Kino-Abend, nicht?" – Im Baseler St. Jakob-Park findet dieses Wochenende zum ersten Mal kein Fußballspiel, sondern ein Freizeit-Treffen für Jugendliche statt. Das Treffen heißt „Frei!" und die Organisatoren hoffen, dass rund 19.500 junge Besucher an beiden Tagen von zehn Uhr bis fünf Uhr in das Stadion kommen werden.

Viele Jugendliche meinten, ihr Hauptziel in der Freizeit ist, einfach zu chillen. Andere hingegen möchten in Zukunft ihr Hobby als bezahlten Beruf ausüben. Peter zum Beispiel will später unbedingt Sänger werden. Seine Lieblingsfreizeitbeschäftigungen sind Singen und Bands live sehen. „Das wird sich nie ändern", stellte er fest.

Nathalie ist eine junge Gymnasiastin, die sich außerhalb der Schule nie langweilt: In ihrer Freizeit ist immer etwas los. „Ich treffe mich gern mit Freundinnen in der Stadt oder wir skypen miteinander und simsen", erzählte sie uns. „Die Freizeit macht mir großes Vergnügen. Wenn man keine Freude an der Freizeit hat, ist das schade."

Johannes freut sich total auf „Frei!" und findet es toll, dass eine solche Veranstaltung endlich in seinem Heimatland stattfinden wird. „Hier wird man viel sehen, viel mitmachen – und vor allem viel zum Thema Freizeit mitnehmen! Alle Informationen auf einmal an einem Ort zusammenzubringen – na, das ist eine lobenswerte Idee!"

Any answers you write here in English will not count, so you must use German words to express your answers. Just focus on key words – but remember it is unlikely that you will be able to copy the correct answer straight from the text.

Make sure you learn the German question words for dealing with activities like this one.

(a) Was findet dieses Wochenende im St. Jakob-Park statt?

.... **(1 mark)**

(b) Wie viele Tage läuft das Treffen?

.... **(1 mark)**

(c) Wie kann man ein Hobby später auch nutzen?

.... **(1 mark)**

(d) Was ist Nathalies Meinung zum Thema Freizeit?

.... **(1 mark)**

(e) Was findet Johannes das Beste am Treffen?

.... **(1 mark)**

Music

My music

1 Read the conversation in a German chatroom between three teenagers talking about music.

Write the **four** correct activities in the grid **in English**.

> Make sure you are confident with the three main tenses before you go into the exam: past, present and future. Look at pages 95–105 in the Grammar section to practise.

Andrea

Im Kindergarten haben wir jeden Tag Lieder gesungen. Jetzt sehe ich mir gern Musikvideos an und bald werde ich auch in der Schule ein Instrument lernen.

Josef

Nächste Woche werde ich endlich meine Lieblingsband live sehen. Ich habe die Eintrittskarten vor einem Jahr gekauft. Ich höre ihre Musik jeden Tag, wenn ich unterwegs bin.

Jasmin

Ich hatte gestern Musik in der Schule und wie immer habe ich das super gefunden. Normalerweise dürfen wir in der Musikstunde Gitarre spielen. Die Lehrerin sagt, dass wir nächste Woche einen berühmten Musiker studieren werden.

		Past	Present	Future
Example	Andrea	sang songs	watch music videos	learn instrument
	Josef	bought tickets		
	Jasmin			study a musician

(4 marks)

Musik

2 Du hörst im Radio ein Interview mit einem jungen Komponisten.

Beantworte die Fragen **auf Deutsch**.

> Learn different parts of words to help you when answering questions in German – *Erfolg* is the noun for 'success', but you might want to use the adjective *erfolgreich* (successful) in your answer.

Listen to the recording

(a) Was muss passieren, bevor Peter nach Amerika reisen kann?

.... **(1 mark)**

(b) Warum findet die Interviewerin Peters Idee positiv?

....

.... **(2 marks)**

(c) Was ist für Peter sehr wichtig?

.... **(1 mark)**

Films

Cinema

1　Your German exchange partner, Patrick, has sent you this article he wrote about cinema for his school magazine.

> In der deutschen Tragikomödie *Honig im Kopf* geht es um einen ehemaligen Tierarzt, der an Alzheimer leidet. Til Schweiger spielt eine der Hauptrollen, während seine Tochter erstaunlicherweise auch eine Nebenrolle im Film hat.
>
> Meine Schwester geht nie ins Kino, weil sie das als Geldverschwendung betrachtet. Sie meint, es ist viel günstiger, Videos aus dem Internet herunterzuladen, aber das würde ich nie machen, weil das gesetzlich verboten ist.
>
> Letzte Woche habe ich im Stadtkino einen französischen Film gesehen und die Geschichte hat mir recht gut gefallen, weil sie sehr lustig und spannend war. Obwohl es auch schöne Effekte und tolle Musik gab, habe ich mich wegen der Untertitel im Film geärgert.

Answer the questions **in English**.

(a)　Who is the subject of the film „*Honig im Kopf*"?

....　**(1 mark)**

(b)　What is unusual about the cast?

....　**(1 mark)**

(c)　Give **one** reason why Patrick's sister does not approve of going to the cinema.

....　**(1 mark)**

(d)　Why does Patrick not share her opinion?

....　**(1 mark)**

(e)　Why did Patrick not greatly enjoy a film recently?

....　**(1 mark)**

> Read the questions carefully: question (e) asks why Patrick did **not** enjoy the film that much, not what he liked about it.

> You have to answer some questions in English on both the Reading and the Listening papers, so watch out for these **common pitfalls**:
>
> - poor handwriting which cannot be read
> - writing too much detail
> - writing two items for a 1-mark question
> - writing only one item for a 2-mark question
> - copying random German words from the text/recording
> - answering in German when you should be answering in English

Television

Television programmes

1 Your Austrian friend, Nadine, has added a section about television to her web page.

● ○ ○

Viele Seifenopern sind langweilig, meiner Meinung nach. Ich sehe mir lieber Sportsendungen an, weil sie immer spannend sind. Im Internet gibt es im Moment einen tollen Krimi, den ich unbedingt sehen muss. Diese Serie verfolge ich seit letztem Jahr. Wenn man schlechter Laune ist, sind Komödien die besten Sendungen. Jeden Nachmittag sieht sich mein kleiner Bruder einen Zeichentrickfilm an, aber ich finde so was blöd.

Write the correct letter in each box.

(a) How does Nadine find sports programmes?

A	Boring
B	Exciting
C	Too numerous

☐

(1 mark)

(b) What is Nadine watching online?

A	Documentary
B	Soap opera
C	Thriller

☐

(1 mark)

(c) Since when has she been watching it?

A	Last month
B	Last year
C	Last week

☐

(1 mark)

(d) For what mood does Nadine recommend comedies?

A	Happy
B	Bad mood
C	Feeling ill

☐

(1 mark)

(e) What do Nadine and her brother like?

A	The same shows
B	Cartoons
C	Different programmes

☐

(1 mark)

> Watch out with multiple choice questions – even if you spot the word in the German text, this does not automatically mean it is correct. Read around the key word to understand fully the context which goes with it.

TV

2 You listen to a Swiss radio phone-in about teenagers' favourite TV shows.

What is this girl's favourite programme?

Write the correct letter in the box.

> There is a good chance that you will hear words relating to more than one of these pictures – your job is to identify the one which is the speaker's favourite programme.

Listen to the recording

A

B

C

☐

(1 mark)

Sport

Sportfest

1   Read the extended writing task and one student's answer covering the first bullet point.

> You will have a choice of two tasks on the exam paper, so read them both carefully, and decide which topic area you feel more confident with. Then stick with that choice! Whichever task you choose, you need to answer both of the bullet points.

Du organisierst ein Sportfest im Sportverein.

Schreib einen Artikel für die Lokalzeitung, um über das Event zu informieren.

> **Guided**

- **Schreib etwas über das Event – deine Pläne und Erfahrungen**

Nächste Woche werden wir im Sportverein ein Sportfest für Jugendliche veranstalten. Das Fest ist kostenlos, aber Besucher müssen im Voraus online einen Platz reservieren. Das Ziel des Festes ist es, Interesse an neuen Sportarten bei unseren jungen Leuten zu wecken. Letztes Jahr war unser Event besonders bei Jugendlichen

> The first point is open enough for you to interpret it as you see fit and gives you the chance to choose details which will show off vocabulary you know about that topic.

> Note the pluperfect expression (8th line): *gehabt hatten*. Always look for opportunities to raise the level of your written work.

beliebt, die im Bereich Sport wenig Erfahrung gehabt hatten. Das Fest hat ihnen die ideale Gelegenheit geboten, aufregende Sportarten auszuprobieren. Unsere Trainer waren wie immer freundlich und sie haben alle Fragen beantwortet sowie Rat gegeben.

- **Vergleich das Event mit anderen Sportveranstaltungen**

> This second bullet enables you to develop your piece of writing, by comparing your event with sport more generally.

Du musst ungefähr **150** Wörter **auf Deutsch** schreiben. Schreib etwas über beide Punkte der Aufgabe.

(32 marks)

> Keep an eye on the word count, and aim to write about 75 words for each bullet point.

> This activity carries 32 marks and you have two bullet points to reply to. You must answer each bullet point, and in a more or less even way. Don't get carried away with one bullet point and run out of time or words for the other one.

> Always try to justify your ideas and opinions, by giving reasons and examples.

> Cut down on errors in your writing by testing yourself regularly on vocabulary and focusing on the spellings in German – there are lots of online resources you can use, or just choose ten words from this page and test yourself on them.

2   Now complete the task yourself, answering both bullet points. Finish your answer on your own paper.

....

....

....

....

....

....

Food and drink

Celebrity chef at home

1 Read the magazine extract about a celebrity chef.

Write **T** if the statement is **true**.

Write **F** if the statement is **false**.

Write **NT** if the information is **not in the text**.

Der Starkoch und Autor von beliebten Rezepten mag es am liebsten, hier am Familienherd für seine Familie zu kochen. „Es schmeckt total anders, wenn ich hier zu Hause koche, als wenn ich unter der Studiobeleuchtung Lammfleisch mit Soße und Bratkartoffeln für die Zuschauer vorbereiten muss", sagt er.

Gestern war ich bei Benedikt Popel zu Hause. Am Abend vorher hatte er schon einen Pizzateig aus Mehl, Öl, Hefe und Wasser vorbereitet. Bei meiner Ankunft hat er erst begonnen, die anderen Zutaten auf den Teig zu legen: Zwiebeln, Schinken, Käse und Oliven. „Das lieben meine Kinder am meisten", erklärte er lächelnd.

„Mittagessen bei uns ist immer chaotisch", sagt er. „Gestern zum Beispiel gab es wegen der Nachspeise großen Krach! Ich hatte eine Obsttorte vorbereitet, aber ich hatte leider vergessen, dass unsere Jüngste keine Ananas mag. Und in der Torte waren natürlich viele Ananasstückchen. Ich musste schnell eine Schokoladenmilch mit Eis für sie machen, um die Situation zu retten!"

(a) The interview took place in an office.   ☐   **(1 mark)**

(b) Benedikt prefers to cook at home rather than on TV.   ☐   **(1 mark)**

(c) Benedikt's favourite dish is lamb.   ☐   **(1 mark)**

(d) Benedikt's family love tomatoes on their pizza.   ☐   **(1 mark)**

(e) There was a problem with the dessert yesterday.   ☐   **(1 mark)**

(f) Benedikt used the wrong sort of fruit.   ☐   **(1 mark)**

(g) None of his children like pineapple.   ☐   **(1 mark)**

(h) He found a box of chocolates to save the day.   ☐   **(1 mark)**

> Be careful you don't confuse an **F** answer with an **NT** one. To be **NT**, the text must make no specific mention of the fact in the statement. Here, the article mentions 'lamb', but it does not give any indication that it is Benedikt's favourite dish, so (c) = **NT**.

Meals

Die verlorene Ehre der Katharina Blum **by Heinrich Böll**

1 Lies diesen Text. Bei Trude bereitet man das Frühstück vor.

Beantworte die Fragen **auf Deutsch**.

> Trude hatte schon die Kaffeemaschine angemacht und wusch sich im Bad. Die Zeitung lag im Salon auf dem Tisch und zwei Telegramme.
>
> Es war gerade acht Uhr fünfzehn und fast genau die Zeit, zu der ihnen sonst Katharina das Frühstück servierte: hübsch, wie sie immer den Tisch deckte, mit Blumen und frisch gewaschenen Tüchern und Servietten, vielerlei Brot und Honig, Eiern und Kaffee und für Trude Toast und Orangenmarmelade.
>
> Sogar Trude war sentimental, als sie die Kaffeemaschine, ein bisschen Knäckebrot, Honig und Butter brachte.
>
> »Es wird nie mehr so sein, nie mehr.«

(a) Wo wusch sich Trude? .... **(1 mark)**

(b) Um wie viel Uhr frühstückte Katharina normalerweise?

.... **(1 mark)**

(c) Wie sah der gedeckte Tisch immer aus? .... **(1 mark)**

(d) Was aß Trude normalerweise zum Frühstück? .... **(1 mark)**

(e) Wie fühlte sich Trude? .... **(1 mark)**

Mealtimes

2 Your exchange partner, Christian, is telling you about mealtimes at his house.

Fill in the gaps **in English** to complete the sentences.

Listen to the recording

(a) Grandma often prepares .... **(1 mark)**

(b) Christian prefers eating .... **(1 mark)**

(c) Christian finds evening meals on .... the best. **(1 mark)**

(d) He is allowed to eat once a week in the .... **(1 mark)**

(e) His family's favourite meal is .... **(1 mark)**

> You are listening for precise details here – read the statements and think about the sorts of words you might need to hear in the context of 'mealtimes'.

Eating in a café

Café Istanbul

1   You come across this review of a café while looking for somewhere to eat in the area.

> ● ● ●
>
> Café Istanbul ist ein neues Café am Markt. Die Kellner sind alle sehr freundlich und das Café ist toll für junge Leute.
>
> Das Essen schmeckt sehr gut. Die türkischen Spezialitäten sind besonders lecke und das berühmte Lammschaschlik ist auch echt preiswert.
>
> Man kann auch einen wunderbaren Kaffee in dem Café trinken und die Atmosphäre ist sehr locker. Leider dürfen keine Hunde ins Café.

> Highlight any items of vocabulary you do not know in this passage – look them up in an online dictionary and make a note of them to learn.

Answer the questions **in English**.

(a) What sort of people would particularly like this café?

.... **(1 mark)**

(b) Give **one** reason why the kebab is recommended.

.... **(1 mark)**

(c) What is the only negative thing mentioned about the café?

.... **(1 mark)**

Eating out

2   An Austrian radio show has done a survey about eating out and your exchange partner, Sabine, has sent you a copy of the interview she took part in.

> Use the introductory text before the activity as well as the questions themselves to help orientate yourself as to what you will be listening to.

Listen to the recording

Answer all the questions **in English**.

(a) What does Sabine particularly enjoy about eating in a café?

.... **(1 mark)**

(b) Give **two** reasons why she does not enjoy self-service cafés.

....

.... **(2 marks)**

(c) How does she justify the expense of eating at a café?

.... **(1 mark)**

(d) Give **one** occasion which is worth going to a café for.

.... **(1 mark)**

(e) How does Sabine save money on her café bill?

.... **(1 mark)**

Eating in a restaurant

Im Restaurant

1 Read the writing task and underline any elements which you think are key.

> In the exam, you are given a choice of two scenarios for this writing task – you need to choose **one** of them to base your writing on. You will not have time to change your mind half-way through your work, so make sure you choose wisely!

Deine Freundin Alessa schickt dir Fragen über deinen Restaurantbesuch.

> Here you are writing a reply to a friend, so use the familiar *du* form.

Du schreibst Alessa eine E-Mail über den Besuch.

Schreib:

- **was du gern im Restaurant isst**

> The first point is a gentle start – present tense, and an opportunity to choose details which will show off vocabulary you know about that topic.

- **was für ein Problem du bei diesem Restaurantbesuch hattest**

> This is asking for a negative issue with the visit – this can be anything from dirty forks, to noisy people or a mouse … use your imagination within the extent of your German knowledge!

- **deine Meinung zu diesem Restaurantbesuch**

> Any bullet point containing *Meinung* is asking you for your opinion. Use *weil* or *denn* to justify the opinion.

- **deine Pläne für den nächsten Restaurantbesuch.**

> Words such as *Pläne* and *nächsten* trigger the future tense – make sure this is what you use!

Du musst ungefähr **90** Wörter **auf Deutsch** schreiben. Schreib etwas über alle Punkte der Aufgabe.

(16 marks)

Sample writing

2 Read this student's answer to the task and put the paragraphs in the correct order to match the bullet points above. Then prepare your own answer to this task on a separate page.

> **Guided**

(a) Im Großen und Ganzen war der Abend aber ein riesiger Erfolg, weil die Kellner alle sehr lustig und sympathisch waren.

(b) Im Restaurant esse ich am liebsten italienisches Essen, weil das so lecker schmeckt, aber ich gehe auch ab und zu gern in ein indisches Restaurant.

(c) Nächste Woche werde ich mit der Klasse in die Pizzeria gehen, weil unser Klassenlehrer seinen fünfzigsten Geburtstag feiern wird und er uns alle eingeladen hat.

(d) Als Vorspeise habe ich eine Kartoffelsuppe gegessen, aber sie war echt salzig, und ich musste sie zur Küche zurückschicken.

Correct order:

1 b   2 ………   3 ………   4 ………

Food opinions

Healthy living

1   Read these blogs by two contributors to a German healthy living website.

> **Ben:** Als ich jünger war, aß ich zu viele Süßigkeiten, und ich trank immer mit meinen Freunden große Flaschen Cola sowie Energiegetränke. In der Grundschule hatte ich riesige Probleme mit den Zähnen und ich musste deshalb meine Gewohnheiten ändern, um sie zu schützen. Meine Schwester ist Vegetarierin, aber ihr Essen finde ich schrecklich, weil ich lieber Hamburger und Pommes esse. Ich sollte wohl einige Kilos abnehmen, aber das gelingt mir nie, denn ich mache nicht gern Diät.

(a) Which **two** of the following statements are true?

A	Ben wasn't allowed fizzy drinks as a child.
B	Ben had to change his diet due to health reasons.
C	Ben doesn't like his sister's choice of diet.
D	Ben has lost weight recently.

Write the correct letters in the boxes.

☐ ☐   **(2 marks)**

> **Mina:** Zu Hause koche ich meistens leckere Mahlzeiten ohne viel Salz oder Fett. Mein Lieblingsessen ist Schweinebraten mit Salat, weil das köstlich und frisch ist. Seit der Gesamtschule esse ich keine Bonbons oder Schokolade – Mensch, habe ich die früher gern gegessen! Ich studiere Sport und wir trainieren viermal in der Woche, daher darf ich nur einmal in der Woche Alkohol trinken. Und dann nur ein kleines Glas!

> German verbs aren't always where you would expect them in English! Check for them in second position in a sentence and also right at the end of the sentence.

(b) Which **two** of the following statements are true?

A	Mina cooks healthily.
B	Mina is vegetarian.
C	Mina no longer eats sweet things.
D	Mina has an alcoholic drink every evening.

Write the correct letters in the boxes.

☐ ☐   **(2 marks)**

Shopping for clothes

Translation

1 Translate this description **into English**.

> Kleider einkaufen kann sehr anstrengend sein, besonders, wenn man keine typische Figur hat. Man kann im Kaufhaus preiswerte Kleidungsstücke finden und auch auf dem Markt. Ich würde allen Kunden vorschlagen, die Kleider immer in der Umkleidekabine richtig anzuprobieren. Falls es ein Problem gibt, kann man die Einkäufe dann sofort umtauschen, um später Zeit zu sparen.

> Read the whole extract through once, to get an idea of the theme and ideas or message. Translate each sentence one by one: the first sentence is the most straightforward, so leave yourself enough time for the more challenging sentences ahead.

> **Guided**

Buying ....

....

You can ....

....

....

....

....

....

> Look at the end of the clause in the German sentence for the infinitive that goes with a modal verb such as *können*.

(9 marks)

At the department store

2 You are working in a department store in Germany and hear this conversation between a customer, Frau Frei, and your colleague.

Answer all the questions **in English.**

> Your answer needs to target the question you are being asked – don't just write words down because you understand them!

Listen to the recording

(a) Why is Frau Frei unhappy with her purchase? Give **two** details.

....

.... **(2 marks)**

(b) Why is Frau Frei confident about the date she bought the item? Give **two** details.

....

.... **(2 marks)**

(c) Why might Frau Frei want to buy something in the store? Give **two** details.

....

.... **(2 marks)**

Shopping

My photo description

1 Look at the picture-based task for the photo and read this student's answers to the first two bullet points. Then prepare your own answers to the remaining three bullet points.

Guided

• Was gibt es auf dem Foto?

Das Bild zeigt ein wunderbares Geschäft, wo man schöne Andenken aus der Gegend kaufen kann. Ich denke, dass die Frau im Vordergrund in diesem Geschäft arbeitet. Sie trägt traditionelle Kleidung, weil das den Kunden gefällt. Sie trägt eine Brille und holt ein Souvenir vom Regal. Vielleicht hat jemand das gerade gekauft und sie muss es jetzt als Geschenk einpacken.

> At Higher tier you have three bullet points you can prepare for and two **!** prompts, meaning you must answer two unprepared questions.

> Your first task is to say something factual about the photo, i.e. what you can see. You could **describe** where it is set, who is in it, what they are wearing, or anything else you can **see** in the photo.

• Kann man in deiner Gegend gut einkaufen?

Leider nicht, denn ich wohne in einem kleinen Dorf auf dem Land. Bei uns gibt es keine Einkaufsmöglichkeiten, außer an der Tankstelle an der Landstraße! Wenn ich etwas kaufen will, fahre ich meistens mit dem Bus in die nächste Stadt und bummle dort durch die Geschäfte. Natürlich kann ich zu jeder Zeit auch online einkaufen, aber ich ziehe es vor, Schuhe und Kleidungsstücke anzuprobieren, bevor ich sie kaufe. Es ist immer ärgerlich, wenn man etwas online bestellt und es dann gleich zurück zum Warenhaus schicken muss, weil es nicht passt.

> You can use the present tense for the response to this question, but think about including more complex language, such as modals, *wenn* clauses and more unusual prepositions such as *außer* (except for).

> The use of the phrase *ich ziehe es vor ... + zu +* infinitive (7th and 8th line) shows confidence in using the German language.

• Was hast du in der Grundschule mit deinem Taschengeld gekauft?

• ! (Was findest du besser: ein Einkaufszentrum am Stadtrand oder Geschäfte in der Stadtmitte?)

• ! (Wie werden wir in der Zukunft einkaufen?)

2 Look at the Answers section on pages 123–124 to read and listen to the student's answers to all five bullet points.

> If you don't understand the question, just ask politely: *Können Sie das bitte wiederholen?* or *Wie bitte?*

> Make sure you don't ask too often: this can break up the flow of your conversation and have a negative impact on your work.

> Use any notes you made in the preparation time to help you when answering your teacher's five questions on the photo.

Customs

How does Germany compare?

1 Read this competition entry for a German language website.

● ● ●

Das Leben in Deutschland

In Deutschland ist das Leben anders als in England. Wir fahren auf der rechten Seite – in England fährt man links. Hier muss man entweder „du" oder „Sie" benutzen, weil das höflich ist. In Großbritannien habt ihr nur ein Wort dafür!

Wenn man in Deutschland nicht alles versteht, kann man fragen: „Könnten Sie bitte langsamer sprechen?" Die Leute reden oft zu schnell! Das denken wahrscheinlich auch Deutsche zu Besuch in England!

Which **two** areas does the writer use to illustrate differences between England and Germany?

Write the correct letters in the boxes.

A	Food
B	Family
C	Transport
D	Forms of address
E	Schools
F	Clothes

☐ ☐

(2 marks)

Different ways of life

2 You hear this interview with a Chinese visitor about her impressions of Europe.

Answer the questions **in English**.

> You will hear the recording twice in the exam, so make notes first time round and then decide on your final answer on the second listening.

(a) What made the biggest impression on this visitor?

.... **(1 mark)**

(b) Where did the visitor experience the difference in problem-solving skills?

.... **(1 mark)**

(c) What does the visitor recommend for people who want to visit China? Give **two** details.

....

.... **(2 marks)**

Listen to the recording

Identity and culture

Had a go ☐   Nearly there ☐   Nailed it! ☐

Greetings

Visiting an exchange partner

1   You are doing work experience abroad and your boss sends you this text message.

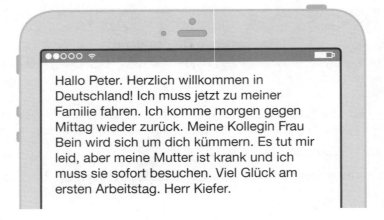

Hallo Peter. Herzlich willkommen in Deutschland! Ich muss jetzt zu meiner Familie fahren. Ich komme morgen gegen Mittag wieder zurück. Meine Kollegin Frau Bein wird sich um dich kümmern. Es tut mir leid, aber meine Mutter ist krank und ich muss sie sofort besuchen. Viel Glück am ersten Arbeitstag. Herr Kiefer.

> Short messages need to be read closely and carefully – every word counts!

Write the correct letter in each box.

(a)   Where is Peter?

A	Austria
B	Switzerland
C	Germany

☐

(1 mark)

(b)   When is Herr Kiefer coming back?

A	Tomorrow
B	In the evening
C	Early

☐

(1 mark)

(c)   Why does Herr Kiefer have to go away?

A	To help colleagues
B	To visit a relative
C	**C**To go to the doctor

☐

(1 mark)

(d)   What does Herr Kiefer wish Peter?

A	Good luck
B	Happy birthday
C	Success

☐

(1 mark)

Greetings

2   You are working at a restaurant and hear customers meeting and greeting each other on different occasions as they turn up to eat.

Listen to the recording

Fill in the gaps to complete the sentences.

(a)   This conversation takes place at ....   **(1 mark)**

(b)   At home, Petra might ....   **(1 mark)**

(c)   This person is .... to meet their friend again.   **(1 mark)**

(d)   Today is somebody's ....   **(1 mark)**

(e)   This woman wants to know if anyone has seen her ....   **(1 mark)**

28

Celebrations

Key to a successful party

1 You read this article on social media about rules to follow when organising a successful party.

> Eine erfolgreiche Party muss man richtig planen. Man muss zuerst entscheiden, wer zur Feier kommt. Wenn die Gruppe zum größten Teil Minderjährige sind, bieten Sie keinen Alkohol an. Sie müssen aber Leckerbissen zum Essen anbieten, also bereiten Sie im Voraus eine gute Auswahl an Brotsorten, Pizzas und Kuchen vor. Sie müssen natürlich Musik für die Party organisieren, aber bitte stellen Sie sie nicht zu laut. Sie wollen die Nachbarn nicht stören! Sie müssen die Einladungen rechtzeitig an die Partygäste schicken – entweder per Post oder E-Mail. Teilen Sie aber auf keinen Fall Informationen darüber in den sozialen Netzwerken mit! Was machen Sie in Bezug auf Geschenke von den Gästen? Am besten schreiben Sie eine Liste, um unerwünschte Geschenke zu vermeiden. Und als Letztes müssen Sie das perfekte Outfit finden oder kaufen. Und wenn noch Geld und Zeit übrig bleiben, gehen Sie schnell zum Friseur.

What **must** you do when preparing for a party? List **six** things **in English**.

> Careful here: you need to write six things you have to do, not just everything that is mentioned in the article.

Guided

1. plan it properly, ...

....

....

....

....

.... **(6 marks)**

Birthday plans

2 While listening to German radio, you hear people discussing birthday parties.

(a) Complete the table in English.

Who is Sabine inviting to her party?	What does her brother think of this?

(2 marks)

(b) Complete the table in English.

Who is Dirk inviting to his party?	What does his sister think of this?

(2 marks)

Festivals

Weihnachten von Astrid Lindgren

1   Lies diese Geschichte aus dem Buch *Weihnachten mit Astrid Lindgren*, geschrieben von Astrid Lindgren.

Der kleine Pelle ist traurig und will nicht mehr bei seiner Familie wohnen.

Beantworte die Fragen.

Schreib **R**, wenn die Aussage **richtig** ist,
F, wenn die Aussage **falsch** ist,
NT, wenn die Aussage **nicht im Text** ist.

Mama ist immer noch in der Küche.

»Mama«, sagt Pelle, »wenn für mich Weihnachtskarten kommen sollten, sagst du dann wohl dem Briefträger, dass ich ausgezogen bin?«

Mama verspricht, es zu tun. Pelle geht zögernd wieder zur Tür. Seine Füße fühlen sich so schwer an.

»Pelle«, sagt Mama mit ihrer weichen Stimme, »Pelle – aber was sollen wir mit deinen Weihnachtsgeschenken machen? Sollen wir die nach Herzhausen hinunterschicken, oder kommst du und holst sie?«

»Ich will keine Weihnachtsgeschenke haben«, sagt Pelle mit zitternder* Stimme.

»Oh Pelle«, sagt Mama. »Das wird aber ein trauriger Heiligabend. Kein Pelle, der die Kerzen* am Tannenbaum anzündet, kein Pelle, der dem Weihnachtsmann die Tür aufmacht. … Alles, alles ohne Pelle.«

»Ihr könnt euch ja einen anderen Jungen anschaffen*«, sagt Pelle mit zitternder Stimme.

»Nie im Leben«, sagt Mama. »Pelle oder keinen! Wir haben doch nur unseren Pelle so furchtbar lieb.«

»Ach so«, sagt Pelle mit noch mehr Zittern in der Stimme.

> Split up compound words to aid your understanding. *Weihnachts + Karten* is easier to understand.

> Prefixes such as *hinauf* and *hinunter* simply mean 'up' and 'down', so focus on the main preposition (*unter/auf*).

> Be aware of cultural differences and customs in German-speaking countries. Presents are normally shared on *Heiligabend*.

* **zittern** = *to tremble*
  Kerzen = *candles*
  anschaffen = *to purchase, get*

(a) Pelle ist elf Jahre alt.   ☐   **(1 mark)**

(b) Pelle erwartet Post.   ☐   **(1 mark)**

(c) Pelle geht langsam.   ☐   **(1 mark)**

(d) Mama weiß genau, wohin Pelles Geschenke gehen sollen.   ☐   **(1 mark)**

(e) Pelle ist sehr selbstbewusst.   ☐   **(1 mark)**

(f) Dieses Jahr feiert man Weihnachten an einem Mittwoch.   ☐   **(1 mark)**

(g) Pelle will dieses Jahr beim Familienfest mitmachen.   ☐   **(1 mark)**

(h) Mama liebt Pelle.   ☐   **(1 mark)**

Home

> Even though this is a literary extract, treat it as any other reading passage. Use the strategies you have developed to help you understand it.

Die neuen Leiden des jungen W. by Ulrich Plenzdorf

1 Read the extract from the text.

Edgar, the narrator, who is in love with Dieter's fiancée Charlie (Charlotte), is visiting Dieter's room, and needs to make up an excuse for what he is doing there.

> Literary extracts often rely on the imperfect tense (see page 102 in the Grammar section) for telling their story, so make sure you can recognise key forms, such as *saß* from *sitzen*, *fiel* from *fallen* and *verstand* from *verstehen*.

Jedenfalls holte sie mich ins Zimmer. Sie hatten nur das eine Zimmer. Im Zimmer saß Dieter. Er saß dort hinter seinem Schreibtisch, genau so, wie er da vor ein paar Wochen gesessen hatte. Das heißt, er saß nicht dahinter, sondern eigentlich davor. Er hatte den Schreibtisch am Fenster stehen und saß davor, mit dem Rücken zum Zimmer. Ich verstand das völlig. Wenn einer nur ein Zimmer hat, in dem er auch arbeiten muss, dann muss er sich irgendwie abschirmen. Und Dieter machte das mit dem Rücken. Sein Rücken war praktisch eine Wand.

Charlotte sagte: Dreh dich mal um!

Dieter drehte sich um, und mir fiel zum Glück ein: Wollte nur fragen, ob ihr nicht 'nen Schraubenschlüssel* habt.

Ich wurde einfach das Gefühl nicht los, Dieter sollte vielleicht gar nicht wissen, dass Charlie mich eingeladen hatte. Ich ging auch höchstens einen Schritt in das Zimmer.

Komischerweise sagte Charlie: Haben wir einen Schraubenschlüssel?

> Use your vocabulary knowledge to help you with unfamiliar words. For example, you know a *Rucksack* is a 'rucksack' (a bag carried on the back); you probably know *zurückkommen* means 'to come back', so what do you think a *Rücken* is?

> Watch out for the pluperfect tense: *eingeladen hatte* (had invited) is not the same as *eingeladen hat* (invited).

* Schraubenschlüssel = *spanner*

Answer the following questions **in English**. You do not need to write in full sentences.

(a) What was unusual in how Dieter was sitting?

.... **(1 mark)**

(b) Why had Dieter arranged his room as he did?

.... **(1 mark)**

(c) How did Dieter create a barrier?

.... **(1 mark)**

(d) Where was Charlotte in relation to Dieter?

.... **(1 mark)**

(e) What did Edgar not want Dieter to know?

.... **(1 mark)**

Had a go ☐   Nearly there ☐   Nailed it! ☐

Places to see

Listen to the recording

Town

1   Two German exchange students have made podcasts about their town.

Fill in the gaps to complete the descriptions.

Answer all the questions **in English.**

Lena

(a) The town museum is open ....

days a week.

> The museum is open Tuesday to Sunday, so you must work out the correct answer from this information.

(1 mark)

(b) You can have a snack in the ....

> Learn basic vocabulary to help you with listening passages – if you are confident with locations in a building, this question will be easy for you and you can move straight on to the next one.

(1 mark)

(c) Photography with mobiles may damage the ....   **(1 mark)**

(d) The town has narrow ....

> Listen carefully to the whole sentence – *früher* tells you this is how the inhabitants used to be. Your answer is something to do with what the town has **now**.

(1 mark)

Martin

(a) There is a trip taking place next ....   **(1 mark)**

(b) The bus leaves at ....

> Read the sentence carefully – this needs a time, not a place, to complete it correctly.

(1 mark)

(c) On the bus, you have the opportunity to see ....   **(1 mark)**

(d) Martin thinks the town is worth a visit because of its

.... and ....

> There are more than two reasons you could write here – but just write one in each gap, as that is all you will get marks for.

(2 marks)

At the tourist office

What to do in town

1   Read this information leaflet from the Bremen tourist office.

> Möchten Sie auch unsere schöne Stadt besuchen? Jedes Jahr kommen viele Touristen nach Bremen und sie kommen oft noch einmal wieder. Warum denn das? Weil diese norddeutsche Stadt so viel bietet: Wir sind stolz auf unsere Geschichte, die tollen Einkaufsmöglichkeiten, das gute Nachtleben sowie schöne Spazierwege.
>
> Sie finden hier preiswerte Unterkünfte, aber während des Weihnachtsmarktes sollten Sie unbedingt im Voraus buchen, weil Hotels und auch Jugendherbergen schnell ausgebucht sind. Erkundigen Sie sich heute bei uns und wir werden Ihnen alle Möglichkeiten erklären.
>
> Mit der „Erlebniscard Bremen" kann man billiger mit öffentlichen Verkehrsmitteln fahren und Sie können sie online oder bei uns im Verkehrsamt bestellen. Außerdem bekommt man mit dieser Karte Ermäßigungen fürs Theater, für Führungen usw.
>
> Jeder Besucher wird in den vielen verschiedenen Museen etwas Interessantes finden. Vergessen Sie bei der Planung aber nicht, dass die meisten Museen montags geschlossen sind.

> Make sure you have revised 'little' words such as *jeder* (each) and *dieser* (this). The more words you easily recognise, the easier the task will be.

Which **four** statements are true?

Write the correct letters in the boxes.

A	The town is in the east of Germany.
B	Many people visit Bremen more than once.
C	Bremen is a new town.
D	Lots of visitors come at Christmas time.
E	You can always find accommodation available.
F	Public transport is not very good.
G	A special travel card will save you money.
H	The museums are not open every day.

☐ ☐ ☐ ☐

(4 marks)

Travel plans

Listen to the recording

2   Hannes is talking about plans for his holiday.

What would he like to do next year? Write the correct letter in the box.

> Look at the pictures – what do you expect to hear?

A

B

C

☐

(1 mark)

Describing a town

Erik's town

1   You hear this audio diary on the radio. What do you find out about Erik's town?

Write the correct letters in the boxes.

Listen to the recording

(a) Erik has ... regret(s) about moving.

A	several
B	no
C	one

☐   **(1 mark)**

> Think about what 'regrets' are in this context – they are disadvantages, so you need to listen to find out if there is anything about the new town which Erik finds negative. You also need to listen for **how many** elements he finds negative.

(b) Erik's new home seems ...

A	familiar.
B	strange.
C	lucky.

☐   **(1 mark)**

> He does use the word *glücklicherweise* but don't interpret this as meaning his home is lucky in any way; he does say he feels he is *im Ausland*, so this should lead you to the correct answer.

(c) Erik's new town is ... his old town.

A	smaller than
B	the same size as
C	bigger than

☐   **(1 mark)**

> You need to pick up on words related to the size of the town, which Erik describes through the number of inhabitants. Don't assume you will hear actual size-related words for the town itself for this answer.

(d) Erik is particularly impressed by the ...

A	sports facilities.
B	students.
C	public transport.

☐   **(1 mark)**

> Cross the items off if they are not relevant – Erik mentions *viele Studenten*, but that does not mean he is impressed by them. You can cross off option **C** too if you don't hear him mention buses or trains.

(e) Erik finds the universities are advantageous for ...

A	older people.
B	teenagers.
C	very young children.

☐   **(1 mark)**

> You won't hear the word *Teenager*, but a teenager comes under the category of young people, so you can infer the answer here.

(f) Erik does not advise a visit to the town centre on a ...

A	Monday morning.
B	Saturday afternoon.
C	Saturday night.

☐   **(1 mark)**

> You won't hear the word *Samstagabend*, but you do hear something which means the same. Always be alert to synonyms in listening passages.

Describing a region

Matching questions and answers

1   Match the student replies (A–E) to the teacher's questions (1–5). Draw lines to link them.

> Your teacher will start this part of the General Conversation, and you need to make sure you respond to the questions with as much detail as you can, justifying your opinions and using a good range of tenses.

1 Wo ist dein Wohnort?

A Am Samstag bin ich zuerst mit dem Bus in die Stadt gefahren, um neue Sportschuhe zu kaufen. Danach habe ich meine Freunde im Café getroffen und wir sind anschließend zusammen zum Skatepark gefahren. Das hat Spaß gemacht, obwohl das Wetter sehr kalt war.

2 Was kann man in deiner Gegend machen?

B Ich wohne in einem Dorf im Nordwesten von England, in der Nähe von Liverpool. Die nächste Stadt in der Gegend heißt St Helens und sie hat ungefähr hunderttausend Einwohner.

3 Was hast du am Wochenende in deiner Gegend gemacht?

C Als Tourist hier muss man unbedingt das Glasmuseum in St Helens besuchen, weil das sehr interessant ist. Ich würde auch einen Besuch an der Küste empfehlen, weil die Landschaft dort sehr eindrucksvoll ist. Es wäre auch gut, an einem Abend einmal ins Theater zu gehen.

4 Was würdest du einem Touristen in deiner Gegend empfehlen?

D Ich würde einen Freizeitpark in dieser Gegend bauen, weil der uns hier im Moment fehlt. Junge Leute würden das super finden, besonders, wenn man den Park einfach mit dem Bus von überall her erreichen könnte.

5 Was möchtest du an deiner Gegend ändern?

E Hier im Dorf hat man viele Möglichkeiten: Man kann im Park Fußball spielen oder nach St Helens fahren und ins Stadion gehen, um ein Rugbyspiel zu sehen. Hier in der Gegend kann man auch ins Kino oder Theater gehen und in der Stadt gibt es viele Restaurants und Nachtlokale.

> Include conjunctions such as *wo* and *weil* in your spoken work to help raise the level. Remember, the verb goes to the end of the clause with both these conjunctions.

Answering questions on a topic

2   How would you respond to the teacher's five questions above? Prepare your own answer to each one, using the student's answers to help you. Then listen to the questions in the audio file here and speak your answers in the pauses.

Listen to the recording

Then turn to the Answers section and listen to the student's answers, paying particular attention to the pronunciation of cognates such as *England*, *Tourist* and *Theater*.

Volunteering

My volunteering

1 Translate the following sentences **into German**.

(a) I work voluntarily.

> Learn key vocabulary across all the Themes, so translations don't catch you out.

Guided

Ich arbeite ....

(b) I help at an old people's home.

Ich ....

(c) I do that every Saturday

....

....

> There is often more than one way of translating the same word! For example, *jeden Samstag = samstags*.

(d) The old people tell interesting stories.

....

....

> Adjectives before a noun need an ending – look at page 89 in the Grammar section to check your endings.

(e) Last weekend we all celebrated a birthday.

....   **(10 marks)**

Helping others

2 Translate the following passage **into German**.

> If you start with a time expression, make sure the verb comes next!

> Once a month, I do voluntary work at the hospital. Although I enjoyed the work at first, I often found the days very tiring. Next year, my brother will volunteer in an animal home. He would really like to work abroad to help animals, which are suffering from diseases.

Guided

Einmal im Monat ....

....

> Know your ordinal numbers: *einmal* = once, *zweimal* = twice …

Obwohl ....

....

Nächstes ....

> The verb goes to the end of the clause after subordinating conjunctions such as *obwohl*.

....

Er ....

....   **(12 marks)**

> Mix your revision up by picking activities from this book to study from in turn – reading, writing, listening and speaking all have equal weight in the exams, so make sure you do not ignore any of these key skills as you revise.

Charity work

Helping others

1 Read the contributions to the donating site, where young people talk about their charity work.

Write the first letter of the correct name in the box.

Write **N** for **Nico**.   Write **J** for **Joel**.
Write **R** for **Ravena**.   Write **L** for **Laure**.

Nico	Ich gebe Bettlern auf der Straße immer mein Kleingeld. Ich gebe sonst mein Geld für Tiere aus, weil sie mir am Herzen liegen.	**Joel** 	Ich finde es schockierend, dass so viele Leute in unserer Stadt kein richtiges Zuhause haben. Am Wochenende helfe ich gern in der Suppenküche, weil das hilfreich ist.
Ravena 	Diese Woche backe ich zu Hause jeden Abend Kuchen, um ihn in der Aula zu verkaufen. Unser Gymnasium sammelt Geld für die Katastrophe in Asien.	**Laure** 	Ich unterrichte samstags an einer Sprachschule und wir arbeiten mit Migranten- kindern, die kein Deutsch sprechen. Ich finde das super.

> Highlight any words you do **not** understand on your first reading. After you have done the activity and read the text through a couple of times, how many do you still not understand? Do you need to understand them to complete the task?

(a) Who is horrified at the number of homeless people needing help? ☐   **(1 mark)**

(b) Who helps people to integrate into the country? ☐   **(1 mark)**

(c) Who raises money for another country? ☐   **(1 mark)**

Geld sammeln

2 Marcus spricht über Spenden für einen guten Zweck.

(a) Wie sammelt Marcus Geld für den Wohltätigkeitsverein?

Schreib den richtigen Buchstaben in das Kästchen.

Listen to the recording

A	etwas Sportliches machen
B	eine Reise machen
C	etwas verkaufen

☐   **(1 mark)**

(b) Wo möchte er später arbeiten? Beantworte die Frage **auf Deutsch**.

....   **(1 mark)**

> Make sure you have completed as many activities as possible in this book across all **three** of the Themes – they will all come up somewhere in the exams.

Social problems

Homelessness

1 You read this article while staying in Germany.

Answer the questions **in English**.

> Seitdem sein bester Freund obdachlos geworden ist, arbeitet Thomas bei einer Organisation, die bedürftigen Menschen in Dortmund hilft. Dreimal in der Woche arbeitet er freiwillig im Stadtzentrum, wo die Organisation eine Suppenküche für arme Einwohner organisiert. Alle Mitarbeiter sind Freiwillige und helfen aus verschiedenen Gründen, aber sie haben Folgendes gemeinsam: Sie wollen alle diesen Leuten aus der Armut heraushelfen.
>
> Die Kantine ist täglich von zwanzig Uhr bis Mitternacht geöffnet und viele Menschen – Männer und Frauen, jung und alt – kommen hierher, um ein warmes Essen zu bekommen und mit anderen Leuten zu plaudern. Das Leben auf der Straße ist sehr einsam und viele Leute finden die Kantine sehr wichtig. In der Kantine gibt es auch immer einen Krankenpfleger, mit dem die Besucher über ihre Sorgen sprechen können und von dem sie Rat bekommen.
>
> Wenn die Besucher in einem warmen Bett übernachten wollen, schickt man sie mit dem Bus in ein Hotel am Stadtrand, wo sie sich duschen und auch in Sicherheit schlafen können, bevor sie am folgenden Morgen wieder zurück auf die Straße müssen.

(a) What led Thomas to volunteer with this particular organisation?

.... **(1 mark)**

(b) What do all the volunteers have in common?

.... **(1 mark)**

(c) What role, other than providing food, does the canteen provide?

.... **(1 mark)**

(d) Give **one** type of professional help offered at the centre.

.... **(1 mark)**

(e) What is a disadvantage of the centre?

Write the correct letter in the box.

| A | no hot water | | B | limited stay | | C | noisy | | ☐ |

(1 mark)

Integration

2 You hear a radio report about Isabel's experience as a migrant brought up in Austria.

Which **three** statements are true?

Write the correct letters in the boxes.

A	Isabel chose to come to Austria.
B	Isabel is dark-skinned.
C	Isabel's parents learned German at school.
D	Isabel's school friends were mostly not from Austria.
E	Some teachers spoke more than one language.
F	Isabel hopes to be a teacher in future.

☐ ☐ ☐

(3 marks)

Healthy and unhealthy living

Although the majority of Reading and Listening tasks will be in English with English answers required, some of them will be in German and require German responses. Practise this style of task with the activities on this page.

Sucht

1 Du liest diesen Artikel über Suchtprobleme in der Zeitung.

Füll die Lücken mit den Wörtern aus der Liste unten aus.

Schreib die richtigen Buchstaben in die Kästchen.

Guided

> Man [C] nach allem süchtig werden ... nach Alkohol, Zigaretten, Handys und sogar
>
> nach [ ]. Unten schreiben unsere Leser über ihre Erlebnisse mit der Sucht ...
>
> 🔊 Mit dreizehn Jahren habe ich meine erste Zigarette geraucht, und seit damals
> kann ich nicht damit aufhören. Mit der Zeit ist meine [ ] immer schlechter
> geworden und ich musste oft deswegen zum Arzt gehen ...
>
> 🔊 Als junger Mann habe ich oft zu viel [ ]. Ich war eigentlich Alkoholiker und ich
> musste jeden Tag Bier oder Wein trinken ...
>
> 🔊 In der Schule war ich total von meinem Handy abhängig. Wenn ich es nicht
> dabei hatte, wurde ich launisch und [ ] ...

A	böse
B	Gesundheit
C	~~kann~~
D	Zigarette
E	Schokolade
F	trinken
G	getrunken

(4 marks)

Gesund leben

2 Du sprichst mit deinem deutschen Freund über seinen Lebensstil. Beantworte die Fragen **auf Deutsch**.

> You don't have to write detailed answers in full sentences here, but what you do write must convey the answer to the specific question. Don't just jot down random words you hear.

(a) Was würde er nicht gern aufgeben?

.... **(1 mark)**

(b) Warum würde er lieber Pizza als Obst kaufen?

.... **(1 mark)**

Listen to the recording

Healthy eating

Online-Supermarkt

1 Lies diesen Ausschnitt von einer Online-Supermarkt-Webseite.

Welche **fünf** Aussagen sind richtig? Schreib die richtigen Buchstaben in die Kästchen.

> ● ○ ○
>
> Heute sind unsere Äpfel stark reduziert. Es gibt verschiedene Sorten, also probieren Sie sofort einen süßen oder einen sauren Leckerbissen! So werden Sie Ihren Lieblingsapfel finden! Unsere Bananen sind zurzeit besonders klein, also sind sie ideal für das Pausenbrot. Wir importieren sie mit dem Schiff aus Spanien, und sie schmecken süß und lecker.
>
> Haben Sie Lust zum Backen? Eine köstliche Torte können Sie mit den frischsten Pflaumen aus Österreich backen! Das perfekte Rezept finden Sie <u>hier</u> auf unserer Webseite. Wir haben grüne, rote und schwarze Trauben für Sie, weil sie bei jedem Alter immer beliebt sind! Wenn Sie außerdem einen Traubensaft suchen, klicken Sie <u>hier</u>. Wir freuen uns, Sie auf unserer Webseite wiederzusehen und wünschen Ihnen viel Spaß beim Einkaufen – bis sechzehn Uhr ist alles um 25% reduziert!

A	Die Äpfel sind heute billiger als normal.	☐
B	Die Äpfel schmecken alle gleich.	☐
C	Die Bananen sind nicht sehr groß.	☐
D	Die Bananen kommen aus Afrika.	☐
E	Bananen sollte man nicht in der Schule essen.	☐
F	Das österreichische Obst ist ideal für Köche.	
G	Man muss Rezepte auf anderen Webseiten suchen.	
H	Der Supermarkt konzentriert sich auf nur eine Traubensorte.	
I	Die Trauben haben verschiedene Farben.	
J	Der Supermarkt findet die Kunden ärgerlich.	
K	Es ist preisgünstig, wenn man jetzt Waren einkauft.	

(5 marks)

> To find the answers, you need to look for related words in the text. For example, statement I mentions *verschiedene Farben* – *Farbe* is a key word meaning 'colour', so although you won't find this exact word in the text, you can look for colour-related words (*grün*, *schwarz*) to check whether this is true or not.

Market stall work experience

2 You hear a radio interview with Raul about his work experience at the market.

Answer the questions **in English**.

Listen to the recording

(a) How did Raul feel after his work experience week?

.... **(1 mark)**

(b) Why couldn't he go straight to the market stall each morning?

.... **(1 mark)**

(c) Name **one** advantage and **one** disadvantage of working on the stall.

Advantage: ....

Disadvantage: .... **(2 marks)**

(d) What could attract Raul to the job of market trader?

.... **(1 mark)**

Feeling ill

Sick note

1 You are working in Austria and you receive this text message from a colleague, Tobias.

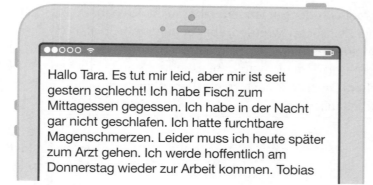

Hallo Tara. Es tut mir leid, aber mir ist seit gestern schlecht! Ich habe Fisch zum Mittagessen gegessen. Ich habe in der Nacht gar nicht geschlafen. Ich hatte furchtbare Magenschmerzen. Leider muss ich heute später zum Arzt gehen. Ich werde hoffentlich am Donnerstag wieder zur Arbeit kommen. Tobias

> Learn key vocabulary for tasks like these – if you know the parts of the body and the days of the week, two of these questions will pose no problem to you!

Write the correct letter in each box.

(a) How long has Tobias been ill for?

A	Since the weekend
B	Since this morning
C	Since yesterday

☐

(1 mark)

(b) What happened last night?

A	Tobias didn't sleep
B	Tobias ate fish
C	Tobias went fishing

☐

(1 mark)

(c) What part of Tobias's body hurt?

A	Head
B	Stomach
C	Back

☐

(1 mark)

(d) When does Tobias expect to return to work?

A	Later today
B	Tuesday
C	Thursday

☐

(1 mark)

Emergency call

2 While training with the mountain rescue team in Switzerland, you hear this emergency phone call.

Answer all the questions **in English**.

Listen to the recording

(a) Where is the caller?

.... **(1 mark)**

(b) Why did she go for a walk?

.... **(1 mark)**

> Make sure you answer this question for 'why' not 'where'.

(c) What situation does she now find herself in?

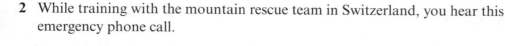

.... **(1 mark)**

> Don't give up on listening just because you are unsure of a word – listen to everything, as you do not know where the actual answer is. For question (c) there are a couple of options you can choose from, so never despair that you have missed your opportunity!

Health issues

Translation

1 Translate this description into **English**.

> Es tut mir leid, dass mein Bruder seit letztem Jahr raucht. Ich habe Angst, er wird mit der Zeit süchtig werden, aber er behauptet, das wird ihm nie passieren. Meine Eltern machen sich natürlich Sorgen um ihn, aber er will Zigaretten trotzdem nicht aufgeben. Seine Freunde rauchen und er ist unter großem Druck, das auch zu machen, obwohl diese Angewohnheit sehr schädlich ist.

> Look through your translation at the end – have you translated **every** word?

Guided

I am ....

....

....

My ....

....

....

....

....

....

> Watch out for dative phrases such as *es tut mir leid* (I am sorry) and *es gefällt mir* (I like).

> Always check whether there is an infinitive at the end of the clause – that changes the meaning of the verb *wird* (becomes) to being part of a future tense sentence.

(9 marks)

Health

2 Translate the following sentences **into German**.

> Highlight any words you consider particularly useful as you work your way through the activities in this book – collect them in a vocabulary book to refer to as you revise for the exams.

(a) My parents don't smoke.

Guided

Meine ....

(b) I never drink alcohol at parties.

Ich ....

(c) I know drugs are harmful.

....

(d) Young people can become addicted.

....

(e) Last year my uncle had to go to hospital.

....

....

> Revise negative forms, such as *nicht* + verb (not), *nie* (never) and *kein* + noun (not a/any) – look at page 88 in the Grammar section to check the endings needed for kein.

> There are two words for 'to know' in German: *kennen* = to know a person; *wissen* = to know a fact.

(10 marks)

Local, national, international and global areas of interest

Weather

Das Schloß by Franz Kafka

1 Read this extract from the text, where a man known as 'K.' arrives in a village.

Write **T** if the statement is **true**.

Write **F** if the statement is **false**.

Write **NT** if the information is **not in the text**.

> Es war spät abends, als K. ankam. Das Dorf lag in tiefem Schnee. Vom Schloßberg war nichts zu sehen, Nebel und Finsternis umgaben ihn, auch nicht der schwächste Lichtschein deutete das große Schloß an. Lange stand K. auf der Holzbrücke, die von der Landstraße zum Dorf führte, und blickte in die scheinbare Leere empor.

Don't be put off by separable verbs in different tenses – *blickte … empor* is the imperfect tense of *emporblicken*, meaning 'to look up'.

Some words might be unfamiliar, but part of the word might be recognisable, so look carefully: *Schein* is a cognate, and you probably recognise the word *Licht*. Look for familiar words and think what they might mean when put together.

(a) K. arrived in the morning. ☐ **(1 mark)**

(b) The snow was just beginning to fall. ☐ **(1 mark)**

(c) K. was very tired. ☐ **(1 mark)**

(d) It was foggy. ☐ **(1 mark)**

(e) The castle was brightly lit. ☐ **(1 mark)**

(f) K. stood on a wooden bridge. ☐ **(1 mark)**

(g) K. was wearing a warm coat. ☐ **(1 mark)**

(h) K. couldn't see anyone. ☐ **(1 mark)**

Being green

The environment

> **Guided**

1 Translate the following sentences **into German**.

> Learn your time words: *ab und zu* (now and again), *manchmal* (sometimes), *immer* (always), *nie* (never).

(a) I always recycle bottles.

Ich ....

....

> Present tense verbs in the 'I' form, mostly end in -*e*: *ich gehe, fahre, esse …*

(b) I never cycle.

....

....

(c) My parents always wear jumpers in the house.

....

....

> Always place the verb in the second position: name/noun → verb → time expression.

(d) I must now separate the rubbish.

....

....

(e) She had a shower instead of a bath, because that was good for the environment.

....

....

....

> Use the adjective for 'environmentally friendly' here – it conveys the same meaning and is a handy adjective to use here.

(10 marks)

Green family

Listen to the recording

2 You hear this interview with Herr Birnenstock, from a family who blog about their eco activities.

Answer the questions **in English**.

(a) Why did Herr Birnenstock start his blog?

.... **(1 mark)**

(b) How does Frau Birnenstock raise awareness of nature protection?

.... **(1 mark)**

(c) Give **one** detail of what each child does to protect the environment.

Complete the table **in English**.

Daughter	
Son	

(2 marks)

Protecting the environment

Translation

1 Translate this description **into English**.

> Die Luftverschmutzung in meiner Stadt ist schrecklich, besonders, wenn das Wetter sehr heiß ist. Der Flughafen befindet sich nur fünf Kilometer von unserer Wohnung entfernt und die Autobahn ist auch ganz nah. Wenn ich älter bin, werde ich bestimmt auf das Land ziehen, weil die Lebensqualität dort doch viel besser sein muss. Wir sollten alle die Umwelt mehr schützen, indem wir öfter die öffentlichen Verkehrsmittel benutzen, anstatt mit dem Auto zu fahren.

> Break words down to discover if they are two or more smaller words joined together: *Luft* (air) + *Verschmutzung* (pollution) = 'air pollution'.

> The expression *X Kilometer entfernt* translates as 'X kilometres away'.

> A form of *werden* plus an infinitive verb = the future tense.

Guided

The air pollution in my town is dreadful, especially

when the weather is very hot. The airport ....

....

....

....

....

....   **(9 marks)**

Eco club

2 Jens and his friend are talking about the environment.

What are their plans for next year? Write the correct letter in the box.

(a) **A**   **B**   **C**

☐   **(1 mark)**

(b) **A**   **B**   **C**

☐   **(1 mark)**

> Even if you are a Higher student, don't ignore the Foundation activities in this book. They are a useful way of checking you really are familiar with the topics.

Natural resources

Eine Öko-Zynikerin findet ihr grünes Gewissen und die große Liebe by Vannessa Farquharson, translated by Gerlinde Schermer-Rauwolf and Robert A. Weiß

1 Read the extract from the text.

The author is worried about the environment.

> Ich lag eines Nachts im Bett, **wälzte** mich von einer Seite auf die andere. Ich war von CO$_2$-Gewissensbissen geplagt, weil ich an diesem Tag allein mit dem Auto – nicht mit der **Fahrgemeinschaft** – zur Arbeit und zurück gefahren war.
>
> Ich dachte über den Kreis des Zynismus und den Kreis der Hoffnung nach, worüber ich gerade im Handbuch für eine bessere Welt gelesen hatte. Der Kreis des Zynismus funktioniert so:
>
> 1. Man stößt auf ein Problem
>
> 2. möchte etwas **dagegen** tun
>
> 3. weiß nicht, wie
>
> 4. tut also gar nichts
>
> 5. ist deprimiert und verärgert, fühlt sich machtlos
>
> 6. kommt zu dem Schluss, dass man nichts tun kann
>
> 7. beginnt, sich zu verschließen
>
> 8. will immer weniger von Problemen wissen
>
> 9. (und so weiter bis zur Apathie).
>
> (Übrigens: das trifft es bei mir im Großen und Ganzen ziemlich genau.)

wälzte: This is a verb in the imperfect tense – note the 't' towards the end.

Fahrgemeinschaft: Use your knowledge of the verb *fahren* (to drive) and *Gemeinschaft* (society) to work out what this means.

dagegen: The preposition *gegen* means 'against' and *dagegen* just means 'against it'.

Write the correct letter in each box.

(a) The author is having difficulty …

A	sleeping.
B	reading.
C	dancing.

☐ **(1 mark)**

(b) When the author goes to work she usually …

A	goes on foot.
B	cycles.
C	shares lifts.

☐ **(1 mark)**

(c) The author's attitude to the environment is …

A	indifferent.
B	hopeful.
C	informed.

☐ **(1 mark)**

(d) The effect cynical people have on environmental problems is …

A	an improvement.
B	nothing.
C	huge.

☐ **(1 mark)**

(e) The author … the group of cynics.

A	belongs to
B	is disgusted by
C	admires

☐ **(1 mark)**

Poverty

Topic: Global issues

1 Look at the photo and draw lines to match the questions with the correct answers.

1 Wer ist auf dem Bild?	**A** Auf der rechten Seite ist eine Tafel.
2 Wo sind sie?	**B** Es gibt viele Kinder auf dem Bild.
3 Was tragen sie?	**C** Die Kinder sehen alle glücklich aus und lächeln.
4 ! (Was sieht man rechts?)	**D** Sie tragen keine Uniform, denke ich.
5 ! (Wie sehen die Kinder aus?)	**E** Sie sind vielleicht in einem Klassenzimmer in Afrika.

My photo description

2 Now look at the picture-based task for the photo and read this student's answers to the second bullet point. Then prepare your own answers to the remaining four bullet points.

Schau dir das Foto an und sei bereit, über Folgendes zu sprechen:

- **Was gibt es auf dem Foto?**

> **Guided**

- **Sammelst du gern Geld für Menschen in Not?**

Mir ist es wichtig, Geld für andere zu sammeln, weil viele Familien in Armut leben und wir im Vergleich zu ihnen sehr reich sind. An unserer Schule haben wir oft Spendenaktionen und ich finde das toll. Zum Beispiel organisieren wir ein Benefiz-Konzert oder wir backen und verkaufen Kuchen und Kekse in der Pause. Jede Klasse sammelt Geld und am Ende des Jahres schicken wir einer Organisation das Geld.

> Your first task is to **describe** the photo in as much detail as you can: include colours, sizes, objects, people, clothes, weather … anything you can **see**!

> Have a good stock of adjectives to express your opinions: *gut, wichtig, schlecht, nutzlos …*

- **Wie hast du neulich Geld gesammelt?**

> Past tense here – but keep it simple. Best to stick to structures you know and deliver your answers accurately and clearly.

- **Wie kann man am besten Geld sammeln?**

> This next bullet point includes a modal construction. Make sure you use this in your answer: *kann … sammeln*.

- **Sollte man Geld für Tiere oder den Kampf gegen die Armut spenden?**

> Start your final opinion with a phrase, such as *Ich finde, Ich glaube, Ich meine, Meiner Meinung nach …* If you want to use a clause with *dass*, remember to put the verb at the end: *Ich finde, dass Aktionen für Tiere (gut/schrecklich)* **sind**.

TRACK
31

Listen to the recording

3 Now prepare your own answers to all the bullet points in question 2 above. Then listen to audio track here and speak your answers in the pauses. Look at the Answers section on page 125 to read and listen to the student's answers to the task in full.

Global problems

World concerns

1 Read these contributions to a youth forum on global problems.

Write the first letter of the correct name in the box.

Write **M** for **Mia**.

Write **F** for **Florian**.

Write **J** for **Juline**.

Write **T** for **Tobias**.

> Highlight words in the texts that are cognates and are familiar to you. You won't need to understand every single word, so don't worry about those you don't know.

Mia Ich mache mir Sorgen wegen des Krieges. Mein Bruder ist Soldat – vielleicht muss er eines Tages kämpfen.

Florian Ich finde die Armut in der Welt schockierend. Es ist schrecklich, dass so viele Leute immer hungrig sind.

Juline Es gibt zu viele Menschen auf unserem Planeten. Viele Länder sind überbevölkert und das ist ein Skandal.

Tobias In meiner Klasse gibt es Flüchtlinge aus Afrika. Sie sind sehr freundlich und wir spielen oft Fußball zusammen.

(a) Who is concerned about the number of people? ☐ **(1 mark)**

(b) Who is concerned about poverty? ☐ **(1 mark)**

(c) Who worries about war? ☐ **(1 mark)**

(d) Who is positive about refugees? ☐ **(1 mark)**

(e) Who has a soldier in the family? ☐ **(1 mark)**

An issue

2 Marcus, your Swiss exchange partner, has sent you a podcast about an issue that concerns him.

What **two** negative aspects does he mention?

Complete the table **in English**.

Listen to the recording

Aspect 1	
Aspect 2	

(2 marks)

Travel

Travelling

(WRITING)

Guided

1 Translate the following sentences **into German**.

(a) My father finds cars practical.

Mein Vater ....

> Work your way through each sentence in turn, making sure you do not miss any words out in your translation.

> Think about the verb ending in the third person (*er*), as you are talking about what somebody else finds, not what you find.

(b) I prefer to go by bus.

Ich ....

> *gehen* = to go/walk, *fahren* = to go/drive

> Use *gern*, *lieber* and *am liebsten* to express activities you enjoy, prefer and like doing most. Just add them after the verb: *Ich singe gern* = I like singing.

(c) The traffic in my town is really loud.

....

....

(d) My sister doesn't like cars.

....

....

> Learn your negatives carefully – they are crucial words which you cannot afford to miss out in a translation.

(e) Last week we played cards in the car.

....

....

> Watch out for the past tense here – it needs two parts!

(10 marks)

Car trouble

(WRITING)

2 Translate the following passage **into German**.

> My mother has a long journey to the office every day. Last week, her car broke down near the petrol station. She has to cycle now, while the car is in the garage. I wish that fewer people would travel by car, as the public transport here is so good.

(12 marks)

Guided

Meine Mutter ....

....

> German possessive adjectives need to match their noun: *mein Vater, meine Mutter* and *mein Kind*.

Letzte Woche ....

....

> You cannot always translate an expression word for word: use *eine Panne haben* to say a car has broken down.

Sie muss ....

....

> Subordinating conjunctions *während* (while), *dass* (that), *wenn* (if) and *als* (when) all send the following verb to the end of the clause. Make sure you do too!

Ich wünsche ....

....

> Do the translation first without a dictionary and then use a dictionary to help you complete any gaps. Try to remember the words you had to look up this time, as you won't have a dictionary in the exam.

Countries

Translation

1   Translate this description **into English**.

> Im Moment plane ich eine Zugreise nach Italien. Ich kann entweder ins Reisebüro gehen oder alles im Internet recherchieren. Ich werde in jedem Fall einen Touristenführer in der Buchhandlung kaufen, weil die Texte und Bilder sehr nützlich sind. Bevor ich letztes Jahr in die Türkei gefahren bin, hatte ich viele Stunden mit der Planung verbracht und das hat sich gelohnt.

(9 marks)

> **Guided**

At the ....

....

....

| Learn set expressions to help with translations: *entweder … oder* are connected words which mean 'either … or'. Use the rest of the sentence to confirm its meaning here. |

I can ....

....

....

| Look to the end of the sentence for the infinitive connected to a modal verb: *kann … gehen/recherchieren* |

I ....

....

....

| Break down words such as *Touristenführer* to get to the meaning as well as using context to help you. This is something you would find in the *Buchhandlung*, which gives you a further clue to its meaning. |

Before ....

....

....

| Watch out for tenses: *hatte verbracht* is not the same as *habe verbracht* – it is a pluperfect form. |

Foreign travel

2   You listen to an interview on German radio about foreign travel.

Answer the questions **in English**.

(a) Why has Gabi travelled widely in Europe?

....   **(1 mark)**

(b) How did Gabi feel when she visited Spain?

....   **(1 mark)**

Later in the interview, Gabi talks about other travel.

(c) Why does Gabi prefer going to the countryside now? Give **two** reasons.

....

....   **(2 marks)**

Listen to the recording

Transport

Emil und die Detektive von Erich Kästner

1   Lies diesen Text aus dem Buch *Emil und die Detektive* von Erich Kästner.
Emil ist gerade in Berlin angekommen und sucht nach dem Mann, der zuvor sein Geld im Zug gestohlen hat.

Beantworte die Fragen **auf Deutsch**.

> **Straßenbahnlinie 177**
>
> Und die Straßenbahn fuhr. Und sie hielt. Und sie fuhr weiter. Emil las den Namen der schönen breiten Straße. Kaiserallee hieß sie. Er fuhr und wusste nicht, wohin. Im andern Wagen saß ein Dieb. Und vielleicht saßen und standen noch andere Diebe in der Bahn. Niemand kümmerte sich um ihn. Ein fremder Herr hatte ihm zwar einen Fahrschein geschenkt. Doch nun las er schon wieder die Zeitung.
>
> Die Stadt war so groß. Und Emil war so klein. … Vier Millionen Menschen lebten in Berlin und keiner interessierte sich für Emil Tischbein.

> Look out for verbs made from familiar nouns to help your understanding. *Geschenk* = 'present' and *geschenkt* = 'given'.

(a) Welches Transportmittel benutzt Emil?

....   **(1 mark)**

(b) Was war der Name der großen Straße?

....   **(1 mark)**

(c) Wer war im nächsten Straßenbahnabteil?

....   **(1 mark)**

(d) Wer hatte eine Fahrkarte gekauft?

....   **(1 mark)**

(e) Wie ist Emil anders als die Stadt?

....   **(1 mark)**

(f) Wie viele Einwohner hat die Stadt?

....   **(1 mark)**

Hamburg transport

2   Listen to this advert for the Hamburg public transport system.

Which **three** statements are true?

Write the correct letters in the boxes.

Listen to the recording

A	The city transport system is dirty.
B	City and regional buses are available.
C	All bus routes offer a 24-hour service.
D	There is no underground.
E	You don't need a car to get around.
F	The city transport system is good value for money.

> If you are really stuck with the choice of a correct answer, use your common sense to help you. This is an advert for a public transport system – is the speaker likely to be admitting it is dirty?

(3 marks)

Directions

Wegbeschreibungen zur Party

1 Lies Lennys Wegbeschreibungen.

Welche **vier** Aussagen sind richtig?

Schreib die richtigen Buchstaben in die Kästchen.

> ✉
>
> Ich organisiere für den 23. Mai eine Party bei mir! Meine Adresse ist Reisstraße 34 (die braucht man!) und es gibt eine Bushaltestelle nur zwei Minuten entfernt. Ihr könnt also mit dem Bus Nummer 124 zur Party fahren.
>
> Ihr könnt natürlich auch mit dem Rad zum Fest kommen, weil die Fahrradwege prima sind. Fahrt an der Schule links und dann über die Brücke. Nehmt die zweite Straße rechts und fahrt geradeaus bis zur Straßenkreuzung.
>
> Unser Haus liegt auf der rechten Seite zwischen der Kirche und der Grünanlage.

> Instructions can be in any one of the 'you' forms: *du*, *Sie* and *ihr*. Make sure you recognise them in a reading passage.

A	Lenny feiert im Frühling ein Fest.
B	Lenny ist zum Fest gegangen.
C	Man kann mit der Bahn zur Party fahren.
D	Lennys Haus ist mit öffentlichen Verkehrsmitteln erreichbar.
E	Es ist problemlos dorthin mit dem Rad zu fahren.
F	Es ist gefährlich mit dem Rad dorthin zu fahren.
G	Lenny beschreibt den Weg zum Haus nicht sehr genau.
H	Lennys Haus liegt in der Nähe eines religiösen Gebäudes.

☐ ☐ ☐ ☐   **(4 marks)**

Sat-nav directions

2 Listen to these sat-nav directions you hear while driving in Germany.

Listen to the recording

Fill in the gaps to complete the directions **in English**.

(a) After the traffic lights, the instruction is to .... **(1 mark)**

(b) At the roundabout, you have to .... **(1 mark)**

(c) In 200 metres, you have to .... **(1 mark)**

(d) The theatre is on .... **(1 mark)**

> Make learning cards for key expressions – draw a direction on one side and write the German on the other side. You can then test yourself to help widen and reinforce your vocabulary bank.

Tourism

Translation

1 Translate this description **into English**.

> Meine Eltern machen oft Urlaub. Sie schreiben gern Postkarten und posten Fotos online. Im Sommer mache ich eine Busreise an die Küste. Ich fahre nie zu einem Flughafen, weil ich nicht gern fliege. Letztes Jahr bin ich mit der Bahn in die Schweiz gefahren.

(9 marks)

Guided

My parents ....

....

They ....

....

In ....

....

I ....

....

Last ....

....

> Translate *gern* as 'like' doing something, so *gern schreiben* means 'like writing'.

> The future is indicated here by the use of *Im Sommer* + present tense. You decide how you want to translate this: 'I am going' or 'I will go'.

> Watch out for the negatives – they both need to be translated for the sentence to make sense.

> Watch out for the tense in this sentence – it is not in the present tense.

> Learn irregular verbs, such as *fahren* (to go), to help you with your translations.

Holiday report

Listen to the recording

2 You hear a holiday report on the radio while travelling through Switzerland.

Which **three** statements are true?

Write the correct letters in the boxes.

A	The accommodation was amazing.
B	The hotel was very big.
C	The choice of walks was disappointing.
D	There were not many cars on the roads.
E	The mountain trip was as anticipated.
F	Mountain weather can surprise people.

> Make sure you have learned your quantity words: *wenig* = 'not much', *viel* = 'lots'.

> In tasks like this, you often have a choice between two statements – decide whether **E** or **F** is correct by listening very carefully to the final sentence.

☐ ☐ ☐

(3 marks)

Had a go ☐   Nearly there ☐   Nailed it! ☐

Holiday preferences

At the travel agency

1 Look at the role play card and read the student's response to the first **three** points.

> **Topic: Travel and tourist transactions**
>
> **Instructions to candidates:**
>
> Your teacher will play the part of the travel agent and will speak first.
>
> You should address the travel agent as *Sie*.
>
> When you see this – ! – you will have to respond to something you have not prepared.
>
> When you see this – ? – you will have to ask a question.
>
> **Task**
>
> **Sie sind im Reisebüro in Deutschland und möchten in Urlaub fahren. Sie sprechen mit dem Manager/ der Managerin.**
>
> **1 Urlaub – wohin**
>
> Guten Tag. Wohin wollen Sie in Urlaub fahren?
>
> Ich interessiere mich für einen Urlaub in Spanien.
>
> **2 !**
>
> Wie lange wollen Sie bleiben?
>
> Ich möchte eine Woche dort verbringen.
>
> **3 Unterkunft – was und warum**
>
> Was für eine Unterkunft möchten Sie und warum?
>
> Ich möchte am liebsten in einem Hotel bleiben, weil das am bequemsten ist.

This is a formal situation at a travel agency, so *Sie* is required.

You have **five** points which you need to **communicate** to your teacher in German. Repeating words from the card with a questioning intonation is not acceptable!

This gives the setting in German – it may also contain vocabulary you can recycle, such as *möchten* and *Urlaub*.

One detail is asked for here – where you are going. Prepare for this by choosing a country or town and stick to it.

This is your unexpected question and it really does not matter what response you give to it **as long as** it **answers** it! Your teacher is not trying to catch you out – the question in this particular role play will be on something to do with a holiday booking, so think about what it may be in advance.

Here you must give both the accommodation where you want to stay **and** a reason for that choice.

Over to you!

2 Now prepare your own responses to the prompts above, then look at the remaining two prompts below and make notes on how you would answer them. Then listen to this audio file with all the teacher parts (1–5), and speak your answers in the pauses. You can then listen to the audio file with one student's answers, and look at the transcript, in the Answers section on page 126.

It is important to concentrate to make sure you hear your teacher's question clearly. If you miss it, you need to ask: *Können Sie das bitte wiederholen?* or *Wie bitte?* But it really is better if you catch it first time round.

Listen to the recording

4 Urlaub – letztes Jahr

5 ? Preis

Speak clearly and with a good German pronunciation. You can practise this by repeating these short extracts after the speakers, trying to imitate their pronunciation and intonation closely.

Hotels

Booking a room

1 Look at the role play card and read the student's response to the first **three** points.

> **Topic: Travel and tourist transactions**
>
> **Instructions to candidates:**
>
> Your teacher will play the part of the hotel manager and will speak first.
>
> You should address the hotel manager as *Sie*.
>
> When you see this – ! – you will have to respond to something you have not prepared.
>
> When you see this – ? – you will have to ask a question.
>
> **Task**
>
> **Sie sind am Telefon und wollen ein Zimmer in einem Hotel in Deutschland reservieren. Sie sprechen mit dem Manager/der Managerin.**
>
> **1 Reservierung – was und wie lange**
>
> > Was reservieren Sie und für wie lange?
>
> > Ein Doppelzimmer für zwei Nächte, bitte.
>
> **2 Ankunft – Tag und Uhrzeit**
>
> > Wann kommen Sie an?
>
> > Am Dienstag um sechs Uhr abends.
>
> **3 !**
>
> > Wie fahren Sie zum Hotel?
>
> > Ich fahre mit dem Zug.

> Read the instructions so you can start thinking about vocabulary and expressions which could come in handy for the task.

> You have:
> • **one** unexpected question to respond to, so think about possibilities for this, and
> • **one** question to ask, so prepare this using the information in prompt 5.

> This gives the setting in German – it also gives you the register that will be used – here it is *Sie* for the formal setting.

> You need to respond to the precise details here – what (i.e. type or number of rooms) and how long for (nights, weeks).

> Here you must communicate both the day and time of your arrival. You can prepare this in advance to ensure you give an accurate response.

> Listen for key words in the unexpected question. Here *wie* and *fahren* lead you to respond with how you are travelling – any method will do!

Over to you!

2 Now prepare your own responses to the prompts above, and then look at the remaining two prompts below and make notes on how you would answer them. Then listen to the audio file of one student's answers, and look at the transcript, in the Answers section on page 126, before responding to all five prompts yourself using the audio track here.

4 Am Abend (zwei Aktivitäten)

5 ? Preis

> Your responses do not need to be complex, but try to make yourself sound German by taking care with your pronunciation – the recording will help you with this.

Campsites

Campsite adverts

1   You come across these adverts for campsites.

Read the adverts and complete the sentences **in English**.

> Besuchen Sie zwischen Mai und Oktober unseren neuen Campingplatz auf der wunderschönen Insel Sylt. Badetücher und Schlafsäcke können Sie hier mieten. Hier kann man sich besonders gut ausruhen, weil die Natur bei uns echt wunderbar ist.

(a) The campsite opens in .... **(1 mark)**

(b) You can hire .... **(1 mark)**

(c) You can relax on Sylt because .... **(1 mark)**

> Ab zehn Uhr ist Ruhezeit auf dem Campingplatz und daher ist laute Musik nicht erlaubt. Es ist herrlich hier draußen im Freien und alle unsere Gäste wollen die Ruhe genießen! Reservieren Sie heute einen Platz für Ihr Zelt auf dem Campingplatz oder ein Zimmer in unserem Bauernhof nebenan!

(d) After ten o'clock, everybody has to be .... **(1 mark)**

(e) The peace is appreciated by .... **(1 mark)**

(f) Rooms are available in .... **(1 mark)**

Campsite report

2   You hear a father talking about his holiday experiences on a call-in radio show.

Answer all the questions **in English**.

> For question 2(a), listen carefully – you may hear the cognate *Beste*, but you also need to pick up on **what** is 'the best' – it is not the campsite! Listen again to get the answer – just writing 'best' will not score you a mark.

Listen to the recording

(a) Why does the caller return to the same campsite?

.... **(1 mark)**

(b) Why are his children not keen on the site?

.... **(1 mark)**

(c) How has their opinion affected the choice of the next holiday?

.... **(1 mark)**

Accommodation

Accommodation choices

1 Read the adverts for four types of accommodation on the internet.

Write the first letter of the correct type of accommodation in the box.

Write **H** for **Hotel**.
Write **G** for **Gasthaus**.
Write **B** for **Bauernhof**.
Write **W** for **Wohnblock**.

Hotel	Bei uns darf man leider keine Haustiere dabei haben. Die Frühstücksauswahl ist aber einmalig und riesig und man hat danach keinen Hunger mehr bis zum Abendbrot!
Gasthaus	Hier sind die Zimmer sehr bequem und haben frische Blumen auf dem Tisch. Das Haus ist schön möbliert und wir haben einen herrlichen Garten, wo Sie sich zu jeder Zeit entspannen können.
Bauernhof	Hier erleben Sie einen originellen Aufenthalt, weil Sie direkt neben den Kühen und den Enten übernachten. Dieser Urlaub passt besonders gut zu Frühaufstehern und Tierliebhabern!
Wohnblock	Mieten Sie eine Wohnung und wohnen Sie wie die Einwohner der Gegend! So können Sie die Umgebung richtig gut kennenlernen. Badetücher und Bettwäsche bringen Sie bitte selbst mit.

> Some German words are formed by combining smaller words – *Frühaufsteher* comes from *früh* (early) and *aufstehen* (to get up). Break down long words like this to aid your understanding.

(a) Where will you feel like a local? ☐ **(1 mark)**

(b) Where can you relax outside? ☐ **(1 mark)**

(c) Where do you get well fed? ☐ **(1 mark)**

(d) Where might it be challenging to have a lie-in? ☐ **(1 mark)**

(e) Where can't you take your pet with you? ☐ **(1 mark)**

Holiday accommodation

2 While in Germany, you hear people discussing where their friends stay on holiday.

Answer the questions **in English**.

Listen to the recording

(a) Where is Tanja staying this year on holiday?

A	Youth hostel
B	At home
C	Hotel

☐

> You may hear these accommodation types in the recording, but which one is Tanja staying at **this year**?

(1 mark)

(b) Why can Kai go on holiday every year?

.... **(1 mark)**

Holiday destinations

Holiday destinations

1 Read this advert on a German holiday website.

> ● ● ● ○
>
> **Urlaubsziele**
>
> Ob Sie einen Badeurlaub oder eine Städtereise suchen, hier finden Sie alle Informationen über interessante Länder und Urlaubsregionen der ganzen Welt. Informieren Sie sich heute über die beliebtesten Urlaubsländer.
>
> Sie müssen nicht weit weg reisen, um Spaß zu haben! Deutschland bietet tolle Möglichkeiten für jeden Urlauber. Egal, ob Sie etwas Aktives oder etwas Ruhiges suchen, Sie werden es in unserem malerischen Land finden.
>
> Wenn Sie unbedingt Sonne und Strand wollen, werfen Sie einen Blick in Richtung Spanien. Die herrliche Küste und die kleinen Inseln gehören zu den attraktivsten und beliebtesten Reisezielen Europas. Die eindrucksvolle Landschaft fasziniert den Besucher – die Mischung aus Bergen, Seen und Städten ist fabelhaft.

Which **three** statements are true?

Write the correct letters in the boxes.

A	The company covers a wide range of holidays.
B	The company specialises in beach holidays.
C	The company only deals with foreign holidays.
D	The company promotes Germany as a tourist destination.
E	The company considers Spain to be a top destination.
F	The company thinks the Spanish landscape is not very interesting.

☐ ☐ ☐

(3 marks)

Beliebte Urlaubsziele

2 Du hörst dieses Interview mit der Besitzerin eines Reisebüros.

Wähl jeweils **zwei** Aussagen, die richtig sind.

Schreib die richtigen Buchstaben in die Kästchen.

Listen to the recording

(a)

A	Spanien ist nicht sehr beliebt als Urlaubsziel.
B	Die Deutschen finden Spanien wunderbar.
C	Das Wetter in Spanien ist wechselhaft.
D	In Spanien kann man sich im Sommer auf das Wetter verlassen.
E	In Spanien kann das Wetter manchmal zu heiß werden.

☐ ☐

(2 marks)

(b)

A	Die jüngere Generation bevorzugt Griechenland.
B	Griechenland ist für ältere Leute ideal.
C	Griechenland ist ein teures Urlaubsziel.
D	Die griechische Küche schmeckt den Deutschen sehr.
E	Die Mahlzeiten in Griechenland finden deutsche Besucher nicht sehr lecker.

☐ ☐

(2 marks)

> If you can't identify the correct statements, do you know which ones are **incorrect**? A process of elimination can be useful in this style of activity.

Holiday experiences

Translation

1 Translate this description **into English**.

> Meine Familie macht jedes Jahr Skiurlaub. Wir lieben die Berge und den frischen Schnee. Ich lerne dieses Jahr Snowboarden. An einem sonnigen Tag ist die Aussicht besonders schön. Letztes Mal ist meine Schwester leider ins Krankenhaus gekommen.

(9 marks)

Guided

My ....

....

We ....

....

| Don't miss out the declined adjective here, *frischen* – it is a cognate!

I ....

On ....

....

....

Last ....

....

| Look at parts of words to help with their meaning, such as *krank* (ill) + *Haus* (house), i.e. 'hospital'.

....

> Read through your translation to check it makes sense and you haven't missed a word out by mistake.

Einen Urlaub planen

> Listen to the audio twice – the reporter has two sections, with each one tackling new aspects. You are listening for **two** aspects and **two** reasons all together.

2 Ein Radiosprecher diskutiert das Reisen und seine Wirkungen.

Füll die Tabelle **auf Deutsch** aus.

Listen to the recording

Was sollten Gäste nicht tun?	Warum?
(zwei Details)	(zwei Gründe)

(4 marks)

Holiday activities

Urlaubsaktivitäten

1 Read the exam writing task and make brief notes of words or phrases you could use in your answer.

Du schreibst an eine deutsche Freundin über Urlaubsaktivitäten.

> The introduction sets the scene, so start thinking about vocabulary and expressions you might like to use as regards holiday activities.

Schreib etwas über:

- **Sport**

> You can use the present tense here: *es gibt einen Tennisplatz und …*
> You can also mention what there isn't: *es gibt aber kein Schwimmbad.*

- **Ausflüge**

> Detail activities here which people can do – use your imagination: *Jeden Montag fährt ein Reisebus an die Küste …*

- **Abendprogramm**

> Maybe include a modal construction here to say what you **can** do: *Abends kann man …*

- **Events.**

> You could add variety by pointing to the future here with a time phrase such as *nächste Woche* + either the present tense or the future tense.

Du musst ungefähr **40** Wörter **auf Deutsch** schreiben.

> Note the length of this piece of writing and divide the words among the four bullet points. It really only works out as one sentence per bullet point.

(16 marks)

> This activity carries 16 marks for the four bullet points.

Sample writing

2 Read this student's answer to the task and put the paragraphs in the correct order to match the bullet points above. Then prepare your own answer to this task on a separate page.

> (a) Abends kann man in die Disko gehen und tanzen.

> (b) Nächsten Monat gibt es ein Musikfest.

> (c) Hier spiele ich Tennis oder ich gehe im Freibad schwimmen.

> (d) Montags kann man das Schloss besuchen oder ins Theater gehen.

Correct order:

1 *c*   2 ....   3 ....   4 ....

Holiday plans

Alexander's plans

1   Read Alexander's letter.

> Lieber Opa,
>
> vielen Dank für das Geld. Es ist sehr nützlich, weil ich einen besseren Rucksack für den Urlaub brauche. Ich werde nächsten Monat mit meinem Freund Markus durch Frankreich und Spanien reisen.
>
> Am vierten September fahren wir los. Ich freue mich schon seit Wochen darauf! Markus hat ein Motorrad und die Reise wird viel Spaß machen. Wenn uns genug Geld übrig bleibt, hoffen wir, vier Wochen lang unterwegs zu sein.
>
> Obwohl wir meistens zelten werden, um Geld zu sparen, wollen wir ab und zu auch in kleinen Hotels übernachten. Dann werden wir abends in einem billigen Restaurant essen, weil das Essen dort bestimmt leckerer als Dosen auf dem Campingplatz sein wird.
>
> Wir werden in einigen Städten ein bisschen länger bleiben, um die besten Sehenswürdigkeiten zu besuchen. Natürlich wollen wir unterwegs auch ein paar nette Mädchen kennenlernen!
>
> Ich werde dir viele Postkarten schicken!
>
> Viele Grüße von
>
> Alexander

Which **four** statements are true?

Write the correct letters in the boxes.

A	Alexander's grandfather has sent him a rucksack.
B	Alexander plans to travel outside of Germany.
C	He hopes to be away for at least two months.
D	He will use his friend's transport.
E	He will only stay on campsites.
F	He will eat out occasionally.
G	He will do some sightseeing.
H	He will send postcards to his new friends.

> Scan the text for a key word to locate where you will find out if each sentence is true or not, e.g. for sentence **G** look for German terms connected to 'eat' or 'food'.

☐ ☐ ☐ ☐

(4 marks)

Summer plans

2   You hear an interview with a student on German radio about her holiday plans.

Answer all the questions **in English**.

(a)   Give **two** reasons Saskia considers America an ideal destination.

....

.... **(2 marks)**

(b)   Why does Saskia think she can stay with her aunt in America?

.... **(1 mark)**

(c)   What will Saskia do if she doesn't like America?

.... **(1 mark)**

Had a go ☐   Nearly there ☐   Nailed it! ☐

Holiday problems

Holiday woes

1   What do these Austrians say about problems on holiday? Read these four entries on a chat forum.

Write the first letter of the correct name in the box.

Write **A** for **Alex**.
Write **L** for **Lisa**.
Write **D** for **Daniel**.
Write **S** for **Sarah**.

> ● ● ●
>
> **Alex** Ich fliege oft mit meiner Familie nach Amerika. Ich finde es immer schade, dass die Portionen im Restaurant so groß sind. Ich kann sie nie ganz aufessen.
>
> **Lisa** Ich übernachte im Moment in einem Hotel. Die Zimmer sind schmutzig und nachts kann ich nicht schlafen. Es ist sehr laut hier.
>
> **Daniel** Wir verbringen eine Woche auf dem Land und es ist sehr langweilig. Es gibt nichts für junge Leute in der Gegend.
>
> **Sarah** Wenn ich in den Urlaub fahre, recherchiere ich erst mal im Internet. Wenn es kein Schwimmbad in der Nähe gibt, mache ich keine Reservierung.

(a) Whose accommodation is unsatisfactory? ☐   **(1 mark)**

(b) Who avoids holiday problems by doing research? ☐   **(1 mark)**

(c) Who isn't happy with the amount of food served? ☐   **(1 mark)**

(d) Who is disappointed by the holiday location? ☐   **(1 mark)**

(e) Who complains about the noise? ☐   **(1 mark)**

An der Hotelrezeption

2   Du hast einen Sommerjob bei einer Reisefirma in der Schweiz und die Gäste beschweren sich. Sie hinterlassen Nachrichten auf dem Anrufbeantworter.

Wähl für jede Person das Problem.

Schreib den richtigen Buchstaben in das Kästchen.

> Put a letter lightly next to the end of the question on the first listening, and then confirm or alter it by writing it in the box on the second listening.

> Check you know what the six options refer to – what sort of vocabulary might you expect to hear for each one?

Listen to the recording

A	die Aussicht
B	das Essen
C	die Technologie
D	das Personal
E	der Müll
F	der Lärm

(a) ☐   **(1 mark)**   (b) ☐   **(1 mark)**

(c) ☐   **(1 mark)**   (d) ☐   **(1 mark)**

School subjects

My subjects

1   Translate the following sentences **into German**.

> All German nouns have capital letters – don't forget to use them when you translate.

(a)   I find maths difficult.

Ich finde ....

....

> If you can't remember the word for 'difficult', change it around and say 'not easy': *nicht einfach*. The meaning remains the same so the translation is valid.

(b)   I don't like science.

Ich ....

....

> Watch out for the negative here: use the expression *Ich mag … nicht*.

(c)   We have geography every Wednesday.

....

....

(d)   Our brother finds art very boring.

....

....

(e)   I received a good grade in chemistry.

....

....

> Watch your word order in the perfect tense: *ich + habe* + item you received + past participle at the end.

(10 marks)

Subject choices

2   Translate the following passage **into German**.

> This year I am learning Italian and French. When we were at primary school, we didn't learn any foreign languages. My class will also have Spanish next term and we will travel to Madrid. I would love to study Latin because that would be useful for university.

> Use subjunctive forms to express uncertainty or wishes for the future: *möchte* (would like), *könnte* (might, could), *wäre* (would be).

Dieses Jahr lerne ich ....

....

Als ....

....

....

....

....

> Express the negative with *nicht* or *kein(e)*: *keine Sprachen lernen* or *Sprachen nicht lernen*.

(12 marks)

Opinions about school

Esmas Schule

1   Lies Esmas Blog über ihre Schule.

Beantworte die Fragen.
Schreib **R**, wenn die Aussage **richtig** ist,
F, wenn die Aussage **falsch** ist,
NT, wenn die Aussage **nicht im Text** ist.

●●● ○

Meiner Meinung nach ist meine Gesamtschule toll und erfolgreich. Die Lehrer sind meistens nett, aber die Kunstlehrerin ist sehr streng und echt mies. Mein Lieblingsfach ist Geschichte und der Lehrer ist sehr lustig. Mathe finde ich ziemlich schwierig und gestern hatte ich Angst, weil wir eine Klassenarbeit schreiben mussten.

Ich finde, dass es fair ist, wenn es in einer Schule viele Regeln gibt. Rauchen ist verboten und das finde ich gut. Aber ich finde es dumm, dass Kaugummis in Klassenzimmern nicht erlaubt sind.

Ich finde es ärgerlich, dass wir so viele Hausaufgaben bekommen. Gestern haben wir Aufgaben in vier Fächern bekommen und das fand ich zu viel. Nach der Schule tanze ich lieber oder ich spiele im Schulorchester. Hausaufgaben sind langweilig und ich mache sie später am Abend.

(a) Esma findet ihre Schule schlecht.   ☐   **(1 mark)**

(b) Die Kunstlehrerin hat blonde Haare.   ☐   **(1 mark)**

(c) Esma findet Mathematik nicht einfach.   ☐   **(1 mark)**

(d) Esma findet eine Schulordnung gerecht.   ☐   **(1 mark)**

(e) Man darf in der Pause rauchen.   ☐   **(1 mark)**

(f) Esma darf im Unterricht nicht Kaugummi kauen.   ☐   **(1 mark)**

(g) Gestern hat Esma die Hausaufgaben nicht gemacht.   ☐   **(1 mark)**

(h) Esma macht die Hausaufgaben, bevor sie ihre Hobbys macht. ☐   **(1 mark)**

Moritz's school

2   You hear a report about Moritz's experience of school.

Answer all the questions **in English**.

> Keep your answers short and relevant. Check that you really have answered the question.

Listen to the recording

(a) Give one problem Moritz's school had.

....   **(1 mark)**

(b) Why was it difficult to learn properly in class?

....   **(1 mark)**

(c) What does Moritz want to do as a job?

....   **(1 mark)**

Types of schools

German schools

1   Read Dajana's letter about school.

> Ich besuche ein Gymnasium mit etwa eintausend Schülerinnen und Schülern. Die Uni nebenan ist dreimal so groß, weil Studentinnen und Studenten aus vielen Ländern dort studieren.
>
> Als kleines Kind war ich in der Grundschule sehr glücklich, weil das immer so viel Spaß gemacht hat. Sie war ziemlich klein und ich hatte viele Freunde, mit denen ich den ganzen Schultag gespielt habe.
>
> Die ersten Tage am Gymnasium waren furchtbar und ich war am Anfang zu ängstlich, denke ich. Das Schulgebäude war so groß und ich konnte nie das richtige Klassenzimmer finden. Einmal konnte ich das Labor gar nicht finden und ich habe eine Strafarbeit bekommen, weil ich nicht pünktlich zum Physikunterricht gekommen bin!
>
> Jetzt bin ich in der zehnten Klasse und ich leide unter Druck, weil ich lieber Sport im Freien treibe, als gute Noten in Klassenarbeiten anzustreben. Ich brauche aber ausgezeichnete Noten, weil ich ein gutes Abitur machen muss, wenn ich später als Tierärztin arbeiten möchte.

According to Dajana, which of the following **four** statements are true?

A	Dajana goes to a private school.
B	Dajana's school has fewer students than the university.
C	Dajana was unhappy at her previous school.
D	When she was younger, Dajana liked school a lot.
E	Dajana didn't get on with people at primary school.
F	Dajana found the transition to secondary school difficult.
G	Dajana finds school stressful at the moment.
H	Dajana gets excellent grades.

> Don't get caught out by 'false friends'! A *Gymnasium* is a 'grammar school' – not a 'gym'!

Write the correct letters in the boxes.

☐ ☐ ☐ ☐

(4 marks)

German school system

2   You are listening to a TV debate about people's opinions on the German school system.

> Listen for key positive and negative words here!

What is their opinion on the topic?

Write **P** for a **positive** opinion.

Write **N** for a **negative** opinion.

Write **P+N** for a **positive and a negative** opinion.

Listen to the recording

(a)   Lina   ☐   **(1 mark)**

(b)   Oscar   ☐   **(1 mark)**

(c)   Amelie   ☐   **(1 mark)**

(d)   Julian   ☐   **(1 mark)**

Primary school

In der Grundschule

1 Lies die Beiträge zum Forum.

> **Liza** Die Grundschullehrer waren sehr nett und lustig. Sie waren nie schlecht gelaunt und sie haben uns tolle Lieder sowie Instrumente beigebracht. Es war spitze, weil wir keine Hausaufgaben machen mussten und gleich nach der Schule konnten wir Fußball spielen oder fernsehen. Ich habe damals gern Bilder gemalt, aber jetzt fotografiere ich lieber.

> **Susi** Die Grundschule war toll, weil ich oft gezeichnet habe. Ich hatte ein großes Federmäppchen mit vielen bunten Filzstiften und Bleistiften. Kunst ist immer noch mein Lieblingsfach. In der Grundschule gab es keinen Stress, weil wir keinen Stundenplan hatten. Jeden Tag konnte man stundenlang auf dem Schulhof spielen. Das war superklasse.

Wer sagt das? Schreib die richtigen Buchstaben in die Kästchen.

> Scan both entries to see if you can identify or rule out the writer first – then read the texts carefully before you write your answer.

Schreib **L** für **Liza.**
Schreib **S** für **Susi.**
Schreib **L+S** für **Liza und Susi**.

(a) Die Grundschule war eine positive Erfahrung. ☐   **(1 mark)**

(b) Ich zeichne immer noch sehr gern. ☐   **(1 mark)**

Primary school memories

2 The actor Waltraud Eckstein is reflecting on her time at primary school.

Which statement is true?

Write the correct letter in the box.

Listen to the recording

(a) Waltraud spent a lot of time ...

A	singing.
B	playing.
C	learning.

☐   **(1 mark)**

(b) The class went to the park ...

A	at the weekend.
B	every day.
C	once a week.

☐   **(1 mark)**

(c) At break time they ate ...

A	sandwiches.
B	fruit.
C	vegetables.

☐   **(1 mark)**

(d) They went swimming on ...

A	Tuesday.
B	Friday.
C	Wednesday.

☐   **(1 mark)**

Class trips

Translation

1 Translate this description **into English**.

> In meiner Schule geht jede Klasse einmal im Jahr auf Klassenfahrt. Die meisten Reisen finden in Deutschland statt, aber manche Schüler fahren auch ins Ausland. Ich würde am allerliebsten nach Amerika reisen, aber ich weiß, dass das wegen der Kosten nie passieren wird. Obwohl ich mich letztes Jahr echt sehr auf die Woche an der Küste gefreut hatte, war ich dann am Reisetag sehr enttäuscht, weil ich krank war.

Remember words such as *jeder* (each) and *mancher* (some).

Careful with your tenses here. The second part of the clause is in the future tense, not the conditional: *passieren … wird*.

Guided

In my school, every class goes on a class trip once a year. Most trips ....

....

....

....

....

....

....

(9 marks)

You often don't need to translate the word for 'the' into English, even though the German needs it. *Die meisten Reisen* is translated as 'Most trips'.

Class trip

2 You are talking to a German student staying at an activity centre with his class.

Which **two** activities is he hoping to do …

(a) … today?

  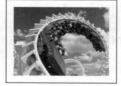 

Write the correct letters in the boxes. ☐ ☐ **(2 marks)**

(b) … tomorrow?

Careful – you need to listen for activities planned for the future.

Write the correct letters in the boxes. ☐ ☐ **(2 marks)**

67

School exchange

Germany–Scotland exchange

1 Read the posts written by German teenagers who are on an exchange programme in Scotland.

Write the first letter of the correct name in the box.

Write **A** for **Anna**.
Write **K** for **Kevin**.
Write **S** for **Sophie**.
Write **P** for **Paul**.

> ● ● ●
>
> **Anna** Ich mag es hier nicht. Ich vermisse meinen Hund – ich komme nicht gut mit meiner Austauschpartnerin aus.
>
> **Kevin** Mein Austauschpartner wohnt auf einer Insel. Wir fahren jeden Tag mit dem Boot zur Schule! Nachmittags gehen wir im Meer schwimmen.
>
> **Sophie** Die Schule beginnt erst um neun Uhr, und das finde ich das Beste. Ich mag auch den Unterricht hier, weil die Labors und die Computerräume sehr modern sind.
>
> **Paul** Ich mag das Essen hier sehr – jeden Abend dürfen wir Pizza vor dem Fernseher essen. Das darf ich zu Hause nie!

(a) Who is enjoying more freedom than at home? ☐   **(1 mark)**

(b) Who is not enjoying the exchange? ☐   **(1 mark)**

(c) Who is living on an island? ☐   **(1 mark)**

Poland–Germany exchange

2 You hear a radio interview with Frau Weglarz, the coordinator for a Poland–Germany exchange programme.

Answer all the questions **in English**.

Listen to the recording

(a) Since when has Frau Weglarz been responsible for the exchange?

.... **(1 mark)**

(b) During the recent exchange, what did pupils succeed in doing to make friends?

.... **(1 mark)**

(c) What were the visitors able to promote while in Germany?

.... **(1 mark)**

(d) Give **one** advantage of the exchange for the visitors.

.... **(1 mark)**

(e) What hope do students from both countries share?

....

(1 mark)

> *Weltfrieden* = world peace; this was mentioned in the introduction to the recording, and *in einer friedlichen Welt* is mentioned at the end. Make a note of words such as *der Krieg* (war) and *der Frieden* (peace).

School events

At school in Germany

1   Look at the role play card and read the student's response to the first **three** points.

> **Topic: School**
>
> **Instructions to candidates:**
>
> Your teacher will play the part of your German exchange partner and will speak first.
>
> You should address your exchange partner as *du*.
>
> When you see this – **!** – you will have to respond to something you have not prepared.
>
> When you see this – **?** – you will have to ask a question.
>
> **Task**
>
> **Du bist mit deinem deutschen Austauschpartner/ deiner deutschen Austauschpartnerin in der Schule in Deutschland.**
>
> **1   Schulevent – was und wann**
>
> > Welches Event gibt es an deiner Schule und wann findet es statt?
>
> > Im Sommer findet immer ein großes Sportfest statt.
>
> **2   !**
>
> > Wie war das Event letztes Jahr?
>
> > Es hat viel Spaß gemacht und ich habe eine Medaille gewonnen.
>
> **3   Schulevents – Meinung und Grund**
>
> > Wie findest du Schulevents?
>
> > Ich finde Schulevents toll, weil sie interessant und spannend sind.

Remember that you have **one** unexpected question to respond to, so think about possibilities here, and **one** question to ask, so prepare this using the information in prompt 5.

This gives the setting in German – it also gives you the register that will be used – here it is *du* for the informal setting.

You need to decide on a school event and when it takes place.

This is your unexpected question, so pay particular attention to the tense it is in. Listen carefully so you can respond in the same tense yourself.

Here you must give both an opinion about school events **and** a reason for that. Giving a reason often entails a *weil* clause with a verb at the end, or a *denn* clause with normal word order.

Over to you!

Listen to the recording

2   Now prepare your own responses to the prompts above, then look at the remaining two prompts below and make notes on how you would answer them. Then listen to this recording of the teacher's part and give your answers in the pauses. You can listen to one student's answers in the audio file on page 127 in the Answers section, and read the transcript there too.

    4   Letztes Schulevent – was gemacht

    5   ? Events – Meinung

School day

Toms Schultag

1 Lies Toms E-Mail über den Schultag.

Beantworte die Fragen **auf Deutsch**.

> Don't ignore the activity title and rubric – they both give information about the text you are about to read.

✉

Ich muss während der Woche sehr früh aufstehen. Nach dem Frühstück gehe ich zehn Minuten zu Fuß zur Schule und plaudere vor dem Schulbeginn auf dem Schulhof mit meinen Freunden.

Die Schule beginnt um acht Uhr und wir haben um halb zehn eine kleine Pause. Dienstag ist mein Lieblingstag, weil wir eine Doppelstunde Erdkunde haben. Die Lehrerin ist toll und sehr lustig.

Ich esse jeden Tag zu Hause zu Mittag, weil mir das Essen in der Schulkantine nicht sehr schmeckt. Nach der Schule gibt es oft Musik- und Sportgruppen, aber ich gehe lieber nach der letzten Stunde sofort nach Hause zu unserem Wohnblock, um mich an den Computer zu setzen. Das freut mich immer sehr!

(a) Wie lange ist der Weg zur Schule?

.... **(1 mark)**

(b) Um wie viel Uhr ist die Pause?

.... **(1 mark)**

(c) Warum mag Tom den Dienstag?

.... **(1 mark)**

(d) Wo isst Tom zu Mittag?

.... **(1 mark)**

(e) Was macht Tom nach der Schule?

.... **(1 mark)**

Teaching routine

2 Frau Grün is giving details about her routine as a teacher.

Which statement is true?

Write the correct letter in the box.

Listen to the recording

(a)

A	The first lesson is at ten past eight.
B	The first lesson is at ten to eight.
C	The first lesson is at eight o'clock.

☐ **(1 mark)**

> Test yourself on times by reminding yourself of the time in German every time you see a clock!

(b)

A	Frau Grün regards breaktime as an opportunity to relax.
B	Frau Grün deals with students at breaktime.
C	Frau Grün works through her breaktime.

☐ **(1 mark)**

(c)

A	In the afternoon Frau Grün relaxes at home.
B	Frau Grün works at school all afternoon.
C	Frau Grün likes to exercise after school.

☐ **(1 mark)**

School facilities

Translation

1 Translate this description **into English**.

> Heute haben wir Chemie im Labor. Ich mache lieber Sport in der Turnhalle. Unsere Schule ist toll, weil das Essen in der Kantine lecker schmeckt. Am Dienstag habe ich eine Dose Cola im Kunstraum getrunken. Morgen früh muss ich deswegen zum Direktor gehen.

> Watch out for false friends! *Dose* is not a 'dose' and *Direktor* is not a 'director'. Context gives you the real meanings here!

Guided

Today, we have chemistry in the laboratory. I prefer ....

....

....

....

....

....

....   **(9 marks)**

> Practise translating by choosing any of the activity instructions in this Workbook and translating them into German. You can check in an online dictionary!

„Der dritte Lehrer"

2 Du hörst ein Radiointerview mit Frau Beton, Architektin bei einer Firma, die kinderfreundliche Schulen entwirft.

Beantworte die Fragen **auf Deutsch**.

Listen to the recording

(a) Wie viele Jahrgänge gibt es in dieser Schule?

....   **(1 mark)**

(b) Wer entscheidet, welche Farbe die Wände usw. haben?

....   **(1 mark)**

(c) Wie nennt man ein Klassenzimmer in Schweden?

....   **(1 mark)**

(d) Welche Personen, außer dem Lehrer/der Lehrerin, helfen auch beim Lernen an der Schule?

....   **(1 mark)**

> Use any of the listening passages in this Workbook to help improve your pronunciation – repeat sentences after the speaker to compare how you sound. The transcripts are all available online to double check against.

School rules

Schulregeln

1 Read the extended writing task and write down some key words you consider useful to use in response to each bullet point.

Dein Freund Kai aus der Schweiz findet seine Schulregeln unfair. Schreib Kai eine E-Mail über deine Schulordnung.

- **Schreib etwas über deine Schulordnung – deine Impressionen und deine Meinungen.**

- **Gib ein Beispiel von einer Regel, die dich in letzter Zeit geärgert hat, und erklär, was du dagegen machen willst.**

Du musst ungefähr **150** Wörter **auf Deutsch** schreiben. Schreib etwas über beide Punkte der Aufgabe.

(32 marks)

> You are being tested here on your ability to **communicate** a response to each of the bullet points. To do this, you need to be secure in your knowledge of German and be able to apply the words and structures **accurately**.

> This piece of writing is all about school rules – ask yourself how secure you are with this topic area before choosing it for your writing.

> Your impressions and opinions are sought here – make sure you express both of these with justifications and examples.

> This has now moved on to the past tense as you need to write about an example of a school rule you **have** experienced.

> Expand your answer to each bullet by giving a **reason** to **justify** your opinion, within the word limit. Try to be creative in your use of language, rather than sticking to simple basic sentences.

> Have informal greetings ready for this kind of task: *Hallo Kai! Lieber Kai/Liebe Julia*, as well as formal greetings: *Sehr geehrter Herr X,/Sehr geehrte Frau Y.*

> Work hard to include the key tenses in writing tasks of this length: present, past, future and conditional should all be used.

Sample writing

2 Read this student's answer to the task and decide which two paragraphs match each bullet point above. Then prepare your own answer to this task on a separate page.

> Check through your written work at the end for spelling and grammar mistakes.

Guided

(a) Wenn die Direktorin kein Interesse an einer Veränderung der Schulordnung zeigt, werde ich eines Tages eine Demonstration mit allen Jahrgängen organisieren. Hoffentlich werden die Erwachsenen dann unsere Ideen für eine bessere Schule zuhören.

(b) Ich schreibe heute über die Schulordnung, weil ich sie unfair und zu streng finde. Weil wir Jugendliche sind, müssen wir zur Schule gehen, weil das Pflicht ist, aber es macht uns keinen Spaß, wenn wir dauernd Regeln folgen müssen.

(c) Warum kann die Schulleitung nicht flexibler sein, was die Schuluniform betrifft? Es würde uns alle freuen, wenn wir zum Beispiel einmal pro Woche unsere eigene Kleidung tragen dürften. Meiner Meinung nach würden alle Schüler an so einem Tag viel besser lernen.

(d) Letzte Woche hatte ich Ärger, weil ich meine Sportschuhe in der Schule getragen habe. Obwohl meine Eltern am Anfang des Semesters telefonisch erklärt hatten, dass wir bis Ende des Monats kein Geld für neue Schuhe haben, habe ich trotzdem eine Strafarbeit bekommen.

Correct order:

1 b + ...   2 .... + ...

Pressures at school

Der Tag, an dem ich cool wurde by **Juma Kliebenstein**

1 Read the extract from the text.

Martin is describing his first day at secondary school.

> Jedenfalls erzähle ich zu Hause nicht so gerne von der Schule, weil Mama und Papa nicht verstehen würden, dass ich dort ständig mit den FabFive Stress habe. Das hat schon am ersten Schultag angefangen.
>
> Ich weiß noch genau, wie ich damals mit meiner Mutter in der großen Aula saß, zusammen mit vielleicht hundert anderen, und **darauf gewartet habe**, in meine neue Klasse zu gehen.
>
> Mann, hab' ich mich unwohl gefühlt. Meine Mutter hatte mich in ein hellrosa Hemd gezwängt (sie sagte dazu **lachsfarben** – topmodern!), wegen des festlichen Tages und so. Die Farbe des Hemdes hat sich ziemlich mit meiner roten Brille gebissen, und außerdem sah es ziemlich knapp aus. …
>
> Ich fühlte mich an diesem ersten Schultag also absolut nicht wohl in meiner Haut. Irgendwie hatte ich schon **geahnt**, dass das nicht so toll für mich laufen würde.
>
> Auf dem Platz vor mir saß ein Junge mit blonden Haaren und Surferklamotten, der die ganze Zeit Kaugummiblasen machte und sie laut platzen ließ. Seine Mutter störte das nicht, aber meine …

warten auf = 'to wait for', *darauf gewartet haben* = 'waited for'

lachsfarben = salmon-coloured

keine Ahnung = 'not a clue', so use this to work out what the past participle *geahnt* means. Looking for connections is always a useful strategy to use!

Which **four** statements are true?

Write the correct letters in the boxes.

A	Martin does not like talking about school at home.
B	Martin is best friends with the FabFive group.
C	Martin went to the school hall with his mother.
D	Martin felt good about his new school.
E	Martin stood out because of his clothes.
F	Martin wears brown glasses.
G	Martin knew he would fit in well with his classmates.
H	The boy in front of Martin had chewing gum in his mouth.

☐ ☐ ☐ ☐

(4 marks)

Future study

Further study plans

1 Read this email from Vanessa about her plans for studying when she leaves school.

Answer the questions **in English**.

> Gestern habe ich die letzte Prüfung für die Mittlere Reife gemacht und ich warte jetzt nervös auf die Ergebnisse! Ich brauche nämlich ausgezeichnete Noten, um auf das beste Gymnasium in der Gegend zu gehen. Meine Eltern glauben, es würde mir dort am besten gelingen, das Abitur mit einer hohen Durchschnittsnote abzulegen.
>
> Als ich jünger war, wollte ich Krankenschwester werden, aber jetzt denke ich anders. Letztes Jahr fand ich das Arbeitspraktikum bei einem Tierarzt so faszinierend, dass ich mich entschieden habe, lieber mit Tieren als mit Menschen zu arbeiten.
>
> Nach der Schule **wäre** es mein Traum, an der Uni Tiermedizin zu studieren. Das Studium wird einige Jahre dauern und obwohl es billiger wäre, als Studentin noch zu Hause zu wohnen, will ich lieber in eine andere Stadt ziehen. So werde ich sicher neue Erfahrungen machen, und ich halte es für wichtig, selbstständig zu werden.

wäre = würde sein (would be)

(a) Why is Vanessa nervous?

.... **(1 mark)**

(b) Why do Vanessa's parents want her to go to the grammar school?

.... **(1 mark)**

(c) What made Vanessa change her career plans?

.... **(1 mark)**

(d) Where does Vanessa want to live when she goes to university?

.... **(1 mark)**

(e) What characteristic is Vanessa hoping to develop at university?

Write the correct letter in the box.

A intelligence   **B** friendliness   **C** independence ☐   **(1 mark)**

Wie helfe ich meinem Kind?

2 Ein Lehrer an einer Realschule erklärt, wie Eltern ihren Kindern bei der Schularbeit helfen können.

> You will hear more details than you need to write down, so use the two which you are most confident with. You might be able to transcribe relevant phrases you hear, or put the details required to complete the table into your own German words.

Füll die Tabelle **auf Deutsch** aus.

Listen to the recording

Was könnte man tun?	Warum?
(zwei Details)	(zwei Gründe)

(4 marks)

Training

Lehrlingsstellen

1   Lies diese Stellenangebote für Lehrlinge.

> German has two words for each job, one masculine and one feminine version.

> Bist du ein freundlicher Teamplayer/eine freundliche Teamspielerin? Bei uns lernst du die nötigen Fähigkeiten, um Bürokaufmann/-frau zu werden. Durch diverse Aufgaben und schriftliche Prüfungen wirst du die notwendigen professionellen Computerkenntnisse beherrschen lernen. Wenn du bei uns erfolgreich bist, könntest du sogar die Möglichkeit haben, in einem unserer modernen Büros auf der ganzen Welt zu arbeiten.

(a)   Wie muss man sein, um bei dieser Firma Reisechancen zu haben?

Schreib den richtigen Buchstaben in das Kästchen.

A	professionell
B	erfolgreich
C	sportlich

☐   **(1 mark)**

> Eine vierjährige Lehrstelle in unserem weltweit bekannten Supermarkt führt direkt in die Arbeitswelt. Hier lernst du, wie man am besten mit Kunden umgeht und eventuell auch, wie man schwierige Probleme mit Kunden an der Kasse löst. Jedes Jahr kommen 40 Lehrlinge zu uns, um hier eine wertvolle Ausbildung zu machen. Bei uns wirst du stolz auf deine Leistungen sein.

(b)   Worauf konzentriert sich diese Lehrstelle insbesondere?

Schreib den richtigen Buchstaben in das Kästchen.

A	Prüfungen
B	Waren
C	Kundenbeziehung

☐   **(1 mark)**

Apprenticeships

2   Working at an Austrian training office, you receive these requests from people looking for apprenticeships.

> You have to write a reason here, so look at the apprenticeship types and see if you can think of the sort of reason you might hear.

Write **in English** each person's reason for wanting to do the job in the grid below.

Listen to the recording

	Job	Reason
(a)	chemist	
(b)	vet	
(c)	plumber	
(d)	banker	

(4 marks)

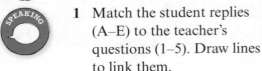

Current and future study and employment

Had a go ☐ Nearly there ☐ Nailed it! ☐

CV

Matching questions and answers

1 Match the student replies (A–E) to the teacher's questions (1–5). Draw lines to link them.

> Develop your General Conversation by giving examples and reasons for your statements, as well as including a question to your teacher: *Ich mag Fußball* is accurate, but it does not make for a flowing conversation. A better way would be: *Seit meiner Kindheit spiele ich gern Fußball und eines Tages möchte ich Profifußballer werden. Wie finden Sie Fußball?*

1 Was sind deine Charaktereigenschaften?

A Seit zwei Jahren trage ich einmal pro Woche eine Lokalzeitung in der Gegend aus. Das finde ich ziemlich anstrengend, weil die meisten Leute im Hochhaus wohnen und ich die Treppen immer hinauf- und hinuntergehen muss, um die Zeitungen abzuliefern.

2 Was für Arbeitserfahrung hast du schon gesammelt?

B In zehn Jahren möchte ich einen gut bezahlten Job haben, bei dem ich in den Ferien viel reisen kann. Ich möchte am allerliebsten nach Amerika reisen, weil ich noch nie dort war und mir das Land sehr aufregend vorkommt.

3 Was wirst du nach den Prüfungen machen?

C Ich habe keine festen Pläne für die Arbeitswelt, aber ich meine, dass ich vielleicht Lehrer werden will, weil das ein guter Beruf ist. Natürlich werde ich zuerst auf die Uni gehen, um dafür qualifiziert zu sein.

4 Wo würdest du gern in Zukunft arbeiten?

D Ich bin selbstbewusst und freundlich und ich finde, das sind wichtige Charaktereigenschaften, wenn man mit anderen Leuten arbeitet. Ich komme gut mit Leuten aus, weil ich tolerant und nicht egoistisch bin.

> Don't forget conjunctions to help your sentences flow: *und* and *aber* are very easy to slip in, and they do not change the word order.

5 Was für einen Lebensstil möchtest du in zehn Jahren haben?

E Diesen Sommer werde ich nach den Prüfungen Kurzurlaub machen, bevor ich im September in die Oberstufe gehe, um mit der Schule weiterzumachen. Ich werde Naturwissenschaften und Deutsch wählen, weil dies meine Lieblingsfächer sind.

Listen to the recording

2 Listen to one student's answers in the Answers section on page 127 and look at the transcript there, paying particular attention to the intonation used, and the pace with which they deliver their sentences: gabbling and rushing or 'umming and ahhing' do not make for a pleasant conversation! Then listen to the teacher's part using the track on this page and speak your own answers in the pauses.

Jobs

Job choices

1   You read this article about job choices.

Answer the questions **in English**.

> You can work out *unerwünschten* by breaking the word down: *wünschen* = to wish and *un-* indicates a negative.

● ● ●

Was mache ich als Beruf?

Jedes Jahr stellen sich viele Jugendliche genau diese Frage. Die Antwort ist leider gar nicht einfach, weil die Auswahl an möglichen Wegen in die Arbeitswelt so groß ist. Und sie wird immer größer.

Die Verwandten haben schon in der Grundschule gefragt: „Was willst du später als Beruf machen, Heinzi?" „Möchtest du mit Tieren arbeiten oder lieber mit Menschen, mein liebes Kind?"

Aus Büchern und dem alltäglichen Leben kennen Kleinkinder schon Berufe wie Lehrer(in), Busfahrer(in) und Arzt/Ärztin, also wählen sie wahrscheinlich einen davon, damit solche unerwünschten Fragen aufhören.

(a) Why do students often not know what they want to do after finishing school?

.... **(1 mark)**

(b) Name **one** area of work young children might choose to work in.

.... **(1 mark)**

(c) Why might a young child be aware of a doctor as a potential job?

.... **(1 mark)**

My job

Listen to the recording

2   You listen to Austrian people on the internet talking about their jobs.

Write **in English** each person's job and their opinion of it.

	Job	Opinion
(a)		
(b)		
(c)		

(6 marks)

Professions

Translation

1 Translate this description **into English**.

> Meine Mutter ist Tierärztin. Sie arbeitet in der Stadtmitte. Ihre Arbeit gefällt ihr, weil sie immer gern anderen Leuten hilft. Letzte Woche hat unser Hund einen Unfall gehabt. Morgen werden wir zum ersten Mal wieder in den Park gehen.

> You may be familiar with the expression *gefällt mir* (I like), so you should have no problem translating it here with the pronoun changed to *ihr* (her).

Guided

My mother is a vet. She works ....

....

....

....

....

.... **(9 marks)**

> Be aware of irregular feminine forms for jobs – *der Arzt/die Ärztin*.

Work experience

2 You are working in an Austrian job centre and some job seekers come in to look for work.

> Check you can identify the photos in German – it is the key 'jobs' vocabulary you will be listening for.

Listen to the recording

What jobs have these people had? Write the correct letter in the box.

(a) **A**   **B**   **C**

☐ **(1 mark)**

(b) **A**   **B**   **C**

☐ **(1 mark)**

(c) **A**   **B**   **C**

☐ **(1 mark)**

Job ambitions

Future options

1   You read this article in a student magazine while you are staying in Germany.

Answer the questions **in English**.

> Es ist heute bei der Jugend nicht mehr so beliebt, auf ein Gymnasium und dann sofort auf die Uni zu gehen. Viele Schüler(innen) bevorzugen eher einen Ausbildungsplatz als Mechaniker(in) oder Klempner(in). Sie finden so was attraktiver, weil sie dann gleich ein bisschen Geld verdienen und sich auch auf die Zukunft vorbereiten.
>
> Einige junge Leute studieren jedoch an der Uni in der **Hoffnung**, in Zukunft einen guten Beruf mit einem hohen Gehalt zu bekommen. Ihr **Ziel** ist es, einen tollen Lebensstil mit einem schnellen Auto und einer großen Eigentumswohnung zu haben.
>
> Es gibt eine große Auswahl an Berufen, die für alle Schüler(innen) geeignet sind, aber sie müssen sich den Beruf natürlich selber aussuchen. Manche Schüler(innen) wollen Parkarbeiter(innen) oder Bauern/Bäuerinnen werden, weil sie meinen, dass sie auch im Winter oder bei schlechtem Wetter lieber im Freien als in einem Gebäude mit Klimaanlage arbeiten würden. Beim Arbeitsamt finden sie genau solche Stellen.
>
> Nach dem Abitur arbeiten manche Schüler(innen) zuerst freiwillig bei einer Wohltätigkeitsorganisation. Sie helfen vielleicht in einem Heim für Obdachlose oder alte Menschen und lernen dabei vieles, was für die Arbeitswelt echt nützlich sein wird. Solche Arbeitserfahrung wird jedem Arbeitgeber imponieren.

> Useful words: *das Ziel* (goal), *die Hoffnung* (hope), *der Traum* (dream).

(a)   Why don't all students opt for university?

....

....

> The questions are in the same order as the text, so keep moving through the passage as you answer each question.

(1 mark)

(b)   What is the appeal of studying at university?

.... **(1 mark)**

(c)   Why should students be able to find a job?

.... **(1 mark)**

(d)   Why might students prefer an office or shop job?

.... **(1 mark)**

(e)   What is the main advantage of doing voluntary work?

Write the correct letter in the box.

A ☐ learn a language   **B** ☐ improve CV   **C** ☐ travel the world   ☐   **(1 mark)**

Opinions about jobs

Views on jobs

1   Read Susi's view about her job in this magazine article.

Write **T** if the statement is **true**.

Write **F** if the statement is **false**.

Write **NT** if the information is **not in the text**.

> Susi glaubt, dass es nicht notwendig ist, einen hohen Lohn zu bekommen. Viel wichtiger ist es, einen fairen und netten Chef zu haben, meint sie. Sie kommt mit den anderen Angestellten im Büro sehr gut aus, aber die Chefin geht ihnen allen auf die Nerven, weil sie ziemlich gemein und sehr ehrgeizig ist.
>
> Diese Chefin schafft eine schlechte Atmosphäre am Arbeitsplatz, aber manchmal kann man das nicht vermeiden, denkt Susi, die schon seit elf Jahren in der Marketingabteilung arbeitet.
>
> Ehrlich gesagt würde Susi lieber weniger Geld verdienen und bessere Arbeitsbedingungen haben, aber sie kann sich nach so langer Zeit nicht vorstellen, sich um eine neue Stelle zu bemühen.

(a) Susi doesn't think a high salary is important.   ☐   **(1 mark)**

(b) Susi doesn't get on well with anyone at work.   ☐   **(1 mark)**

(c) Her boss has worked there longer than Susi.   ☐   **(1 mark)**

(d) Her boss is not very nice.   ☐   **(1 mark)**

(e) Susi has worked there for over ten years.   ☐   **(1 mark)**

(f) Susi works in accounts.   ☐   **(1 mark)**

(g) Susi prefers to go abroad in the holidays.   ☐   **(1 mark)**

(h) Susi can't be bothered to look for a new job.   ☐   **(1 mark)**

A new job

2   Listen to Ben talking about his new job.

Fill in the gaps to complete the sentences.

Answer all parts of the question **in English**.

> You won't get any marks for writing German words here, so make sure you work out your answers in English.

Listen to the recording

(a) Ben is working in .... **(1 mark)**

(b) His boss is .... **(1 mark)**

(c) Ben is entitled to.. **(1 mark)**

(d) Ben considers his job good because... **(1 mark)**

Job adverts

Restaurant job advert

1 You are looking for a job in Germany and come across this advert online.

> ### Bewerben Sie sich heute bei uns!
>
> Sind Sie fleißig und freundlich? Sie möchten in einem modernen Restaurant mit tollen Kollegen und unter guten Arbeitsbedingungen arbeiten?
>
> Wir suchen Kellner/innen für unser neu eröffnetes italienisches Restaurant neben dem Dom. Erfahrung ist nicht notwendig.
>
> Wir sind stolz auf unseren internationalen Restaurantbetrieb und Ihr Ziel als Kellner/in wird es sein, unsere Kunden immer nach bestem Können zu bedienen.

> Don't be put off by *Können* used as a noun here – it just means 'ability'.

Answer the questions **in English**.

> Each question refers to each paragraph here.

(a) Name **one** advantage of this job.

.... **(1 mark)**

(b) Where is the restaurant situated?

.... **(1 mark)**

(c) What will the role involve?

.... **(1 mark)**

A summer job

2 Your exchange partner, Emilie, has sent you a podcast about her summer job.

> Read the statements first and then follow them closely with the recording – they follow the same order as the sentences you hear.

Which **three** statements are true?

Listen to the recording

Write the correct letters in the boxes.

A	Emilie wants to work in a travel agency.
B	Emilie spent lots of money on her trip to Paris.
C	Emilie enjoyed her job last year.
D	Emilie is unhappy about the working hours at a shop.
E	Emilie wants to visit other cafés to find a job.
F	Emilie lacks confidence to ask at other cafés for a job.

☐ ☐ ☐   **(3 marks)**

Applying for a job

> Don't just write the first thing which comes into your head when you hear 'Job search' – you need to tailor your writing to match the bullet points.

Jobsuche

1 Read the writing task and underline any elements which you think are key.

Dein Freund Sergio stellt dir Fragen über deine Arbeitssuche. Du schreibst Sergio eine E-Mail über die Arbeit.

> You need to read this so you know the set-up of the task. Here you are answering questions sent by a friend.

Schreib:

- **was für eine Stelle du suchst**

> Use vocabulary you are confident of here – remember, German has different forms for masculine and feminine jobs: *der Lehrer/die Lehrerin*.

- **welche Jobs du schon gemacht hast**

> Use the past tense here – you can use the perfect (*haben/ sein* + past participle) and the imperfect (*war/hatte*).

- **warum die Stelle für dich ideal sein wird**

> The question word *warum* means 'why' – knowing your question words is vital for all the exam papers!

- **was dir an der Arbeit gefällt.**

> You are writing about positive aspects here, so adjectives such as *prima*, *interessant* and *toll* could come in handy.

Du musst ungefähr **90** Wörter **auf Deutsch** schreiben. Schreib etwas über alle Punkte der Aufgabe.

(16 marks)

> Practise writing tasks as you revise so you know approximately how many lines your handwriting takes to reach 90 words.

2 Read this student's answer to the task and put the paragraphs in the correct order to match the bullet points above. Then prepare your own answer to this task on a separate page.

 Guided

(a) Letztes Jahr habe ich im Sportverein gearbeitet, aber dieses Jahr gibt es leider keine Ferienjobs dort.

(b) Wenn die Arbeit draußen ist, finde ich das besser, als drinnen zu arbeiten. Ich würde deshalb nicht gern in einem Büro arbeiten.

(c) Ich bewerbe mich im Moment um einen Job als Bademeister im Freibad in der Stadtmitte.

> Adding details to the bullet points (where, when, how) will help to ensure you reach the word count. Here, the student has said where the pool is.

(d) Diese Stelle würde mir sehr gut passen, weil wir im Sommer nicht in den Urlaub fahren werden. Deshalb könnte ich dann viel arbeiten.

> Use the Grammar section at the back of this book to double check you are confident with the different points of grammar while you are revising for writing skills.

Correct order:

1   *c*   2   3   4   ....

Job interview

At the job centre

1 Look at the role play card and read the student's response to the first **three** points.

> Don't overcomplicate your answers; the role play is the opening part of the speaking exam and there is plenty of opportunity elsewhere for showing off your German to its full extent!

Topic: Future plans

Instructions to candidates:

Your teacher will play the part of the job centre manager and will speak first.

You should address the manager as *Sie*.

When you see this – **!** – you will have to respond to something you have not prepared.

When you see this – **?** – you will have to ask a question.

Task

Sie sind in Deutschland und suchen einen Job. Sie sprechen mit dem Manager/der Managerin beim Arbeitsamt.

1 Jobsuche – was

> Was für einen Job suchen Sie?

> Ich suche einen Job als Babysitterin.

2 Job – wann

> Wann wollen Sie arbeiten?

> Ich will im Sommer arbeiten.

3 !

> Wo arbeiten Sie im Moment?

> Im Restaurant.

> Use your preparation time fully to cover and prepare for each of the **five** bullet points – your aim is to deliver accurate German!

> Remember: do not simply repeat the words in the task below.

> This is a formal role play – the *Sie* form will be used throughout.

> You need to respond with precise details here.

> Here you need to say **when** you want to work (month, season, now).

> Make sure you know your question words in German – turn to page 106 of the Grammar section now to check.

Over to you!

2 Now prepare your own responses to the prompts above, then look at the remaining two prompts below and make notes on how you would answer them. Then listen to the audio file here and respond to the questions in the pauses. You can then listen to one student's answers, and look at the transcript, in the Answers section on page 128.

4 Job – Grund

5 ? Geld

Part-time jobs

Meine Freunde

1 Lies Richards Blogeintrag.

Welche **sechs** Aussagen sind richtig?

Schreib die richtigen Buchstaben in die Kästchen.

> The demonstrative article *dieser* takes the same endings as *der* and means 'this', just as *jener* means 'that'.

● ○ ○ ○

Mina trägt jeden Tag Zeitungen aus, aber sie findet es echt schwer, weil sie so früh aufstehen muss. Sie ist ein Nachtmensch! Warum macht sie also diesen Job? Sie braucht das Geld für den Sommerurlaub.

Sonnabends sieht man **Felix** bei der Arbeit in einem Supermarkt. Es macht ihm viel Spaß, obwohl er dann abends zu Hause sehr müde ist, weil die Arbeitszeiten lang sind. Das Beste ist, wenn er an der Kasse arbeiten darf, weil er sehr gern mit den Kunden spricht.

Mehmet hilft seinem Onkel, der ein türkisches Restaurant in der Stadtmitte besitzt. Seit letztem Wochenende darf er als Kellner im Speisesaal arbeiten und das findet er sehr interessant, obwohl die Kunden ihm manchmal auf die Nerven gehen.

A	Mina findet ihren Job anstrengend.
B	Mina steht gern früh auf.
C	Mina findet die Nächte besser als die Vormittage.
D	Mina spart für die Ferien.
E	Felix arbeitet das ganze Wochenende.
F	Felix findet den Job ermüdend.
G	Felix findet Kontakt mit den Kunden stressig.
H	Felix arbeitet nie mit Geld.
I	Felix arbeitet gern mit Leuten.
J	Mehmets Onkel ist fünfzig Jahre alt.
K	Mehmet arbeitet in der Küche.
L	Mehmet findet den Job positiv und negativ.

> You can discard any statements you know to be untrue or which are not mentioned in the blog.

☐ ☐ ☐ ☐ ☐ ☐

(6 marks)

Work for teenagers

2 You hear a radio report with Frau Wyss advising teenagers about working. What does she say?

> Double check the rubric to make sure you are answering these questions in the correct language.

Answer all the questions **in English**.

Listen to the recording

(a) At what age does a teenager no longer count as a minor? .... **(1 mark)**

(b) Mention **two** jobs you can do when you are 13.

....

.... **(2 marks)**

(c) How long can you work once you are 15 if you have left school?

.... **(1 mark)**

> Keep revising your numbers in German so they don't trip you up in any of the exams.

Gender and plurals

In the nominative, German definite articles are either *der* (masculine), *die* (feminine) or *das* (neuter). *der / die / das* = the

der Hund   **die** Katze   **das** Kaninchen

1 Circle the correct article.

(a) der / die / das Abfalleimer (*m.*)

(b) der / die / das Kino (*n.*)

(c) der / die / das Krankenschwester (*f.*)

(d) der / die / das Rucksack (*m.*)

(e) der / die / das Handy (*n.*)

(f) der / die / das Restaurant (*n.*)

(g) der / die / das Autobahn (*f.*)

(h) der / die / das Sportlehrer (*m.*)

(i) der / die / das Umwelt (*f.*)

2 Complete each sentence with *der*, *die* or *das*.

(a) .... Haus ist modern. (*n.*)

(b) .... Schüler heißt Max. (*m.*)

(c) .... Schülerin heißt Demet. (*f.*)

(d) .... Computer ist kaputt. (*m.*)

(e) .... Zug fährt langsam. (*m.*)

(f) .... Bank ist geschlossen. (*f.*)

(g) .... Zeitung kostet 1 Euro. (*f.*)

(h) .... Buch ist langweilig. (*n.*)

In the accusative, the article *der* changes to *den* (masculine), but *die* and *das* don't change.

	m.	*f.*	*n.*	*pl.*
Accusative	**den**	die	das	die

Wir mögen **den** Sportlehrer.

3 Write in *den*, *die* or *das*.

(a) Wir haben .... Pizza gegessen. (*f.*)

(b) Wir können .... Krankenhaus sehen. (*n.*)

(c) Ich mache .... Hausaufgabe. (*f.*)

(d) Vati kauft .... Pullover. (*m.*)

(e) Liest du .... Buch? (*n.*)

(f) Ich wasche .... Wagen. (*m.*)

German plurals come in many forms. The most common ones are *–e* and *–n*, but many are irregular, maybe adding an umlaut or simply staying the same.

(S) Brief   ⟶   (P) Brief**e**

(S) Tasse   ⟶   (P) Tasse**n**

(S) Teller   ⟶   (P) Teller

(S) Glas   ⟶   (P) Gl**ä**s**er**

4 Write **S** if the noun is singular and **P** if it is plural. If it could be either, put **E**.

Haus .... , Buch .... , Männer .... , Autos .... , Häuser .... , Supermarkt .... ,

Tisch .... , Mann .... , Supermärkte .... , Tische .... , Handys .... ,

Zimmer .... , Bilder .... , Computer ....

Cases and prepositions

Prepositions which trigger a change to the accusative are: *bis, durch, entlang* (after the noun), *für, gegen, ohne* and *um*.

	m.	f.	n.	pl.
Nominative	der	die	das	die
Accusative	den	die	das	die
Nominative	ein	eine	ein	(keine)
Accusative	einen	eine	ein	(keine)

1 Write in *den, die, das, einen, eine* or *ein*.

(a) um .... Ecke (*round the corner*) (*f.*)

(b) durch .... Stadt (*through the town*) (*f.*)

(c) ohne .... Auto (*without a car*) (*n.*)

(d) für .... Schule (*for the school*) (*f.*)

(e) für .... Freund (*for a friend*) (*m.*)

(f) gegen .... Wand (*against the wall*) (*f.*)

(g) durch .... Wald (*through a wood*) (*m.*)

(h) .... Straße entlang (*along the road*) (*f.*)

Prepositions which trigger a change to the dative are: *aus, außer, bei, gegenüber, mit, nach, seit, von* and *zu*.

	m.	f.	n.	pl.
Nominative	der	die	das	die
Dative	dem	der	dem	den
Nominative	ein	eine	ein	(keine)
Dative	einem	einer	einem	(keinen)

2 Write in *dem, der, einem* or *einer*.

(a) mit .... Bus (*by bus*) (*m.*)

(b) seit .... Sommer (*since the summer*) (*m.*)

(c) zu .... Bank (*to the bank*) (*f.*)

(d) nach .... Party (*after the party*) (*f.*)

(e) bei .... Freund (*at a friend's house*) (*m.*)

(f) von .... Onkel (*from an uncle*) (*m.*)

(g) gegenüber .... Tankstelle (*opposite the petrol station*) (*f.*)

(h) außer .... Lehrerin (*apart from the teacher*) (*f.*)

(i) aus.....Raum (*out of the room*) (*m.*)

A few prepositions trigger a change to the genitive, for example: *trotz, wegen* and *während*

	m.	f.	n.	pl.
Nominative	der	die	das	die
Genitive	des	der	des	der
Nominative	ein	eine	ein	(keine)
Genitive	eines	einer	eines	(keiner)

3 Write in *der* or *des*.

(a) wegen .... Wetters (*because of the weather*) (*n.*)

(b) während .... Stunde (*during the lesson*) (*f.*)

(c) trotz .... Regens (*despite the rain*) (*m.*)

Prepositions with accusative or dative

These prepositions trigger a change to the accusative if there is **movement towards** a place, or the dative if there is **no movement**:

an (on, at)	*auf* (on)	*hinter* (behind)	*in* (in)	*neben* (next to)
über (over, above)	*unter* (under)	*vor* (in front of)	*zwischen* (between)	

See page 86 for the accusative and dative forms of articles.

1 Circle the correct article.

(a) Wir fahren in **der** / **die** Stadt. (*f.*)

(b) Meine Schwester ist in **der** / **die** Schule. (*f.*)

(c) Das Essen steht auf **den** / **dem** Tisch. (*m.*)

(d) Ich steige auf **die** / **der** Mauer. (*f.*)

(e) Wir hängen das Bild an **der** / **die** Wand. (*f.*)

(f) Jetzt ist das Bild an **der** / **die** Wand. (*f.*)

(g) Die Katze läuft hinter **einen** / **einem** Schrank. (*m.*)

(h) Wo ist die Katze jetzt? Hinter **den** / **dem** Schrank. (*m.*)

(i) Die Bäckerei steht zwischen **einem** / **einen** Supermarkt (*m.*) und **einer** / **eine** Post. (*f.*)

(j) Das Flugzeug fliegt über **die** / **der** Stadt. (*f.*)

(k) Ich stelle die Flaschen in **dem** / **den** Schrank. (*m.*)

(l) Der Bus steht an **der** / **die** Haltestelle. (*f.*)

Some verbs work with a preposition which is followed by the accusative.

2 Circle the correct article. Then translate the sentences into English.

(a) Die Kinder streiten sich über **das** / **dem** Fernsehprogramm. (*n.*)

....

(b) Wir freuen uns auf **das** / **dem** Fest. (*n.*)

....

(c) Ich ärgere mich oft über **der** / **die** Arbeit. (*f.*)

....

(d) Martin hat sich an **der** / **die** Sonne gewöhnt. (*f.*)

....

(e) Wie lange warten Sie auf **der** / **die** Straßenbahn? (*f.*)

....

Certain special phrases have a preposition followed by either the accusative or the dative. You have to learn these.

3 Draw lines to link the German and English phrases.

1 auf dem Land   A *on the internet*

2 vor allem   B *on the right*

3 auf die Nerven   C *in the country*

4 auf der rechten Seite   D *on (someone's) nerves*

5 im Internet   E *above all*

Dieser / jeder, kein / mein

Dieser (this), *jener* (that) and *jeder* (each/every) follow the pattern of *der, die, das*.

	m.	*f.*	*n.*	*pl.*
Nominative	dieser	diese	dieses	diese
Accusative	diesen	diese	dieses	diese
Dative	diesem	dieser	diesem	diesen

1 Add the endings.

   (a) *this man*   dies......... Mann (*m.*)

   (b) *with this man*   mit dies......... Mann (*m.*)

   (c) *this woman*   dies......... Frau (*f.*)

   (d) *for this woman*   für dies......... Frau (*f.*)

   (e) *every animal*   jed......... Tier (*n.*)

   (f) *on that animal*   auf jen......... Tier (*n.*)

Kein, mein, dein, sein, ihr, unser, euer (eure) and *Ihr* follow the pattern of *ein*.

	m.	*f.*	*n.*	*pl.*
Nominative	kein	keine	kein	keine
Accusative	keinen	keine	kein	keine
Dative	keinem	keiner	keinem	keinen

2 Complete the words with the correct ending, where necessary.

   (a) Unser......... Schwester heißt Monika. (*f.*)

   (b) Ich habe kein......... Bruder. (*m.*)

   (c) Mein......... Schule ist nicht sehr groß. (*f.*)

   (d) Hast du dein......... Laptop vergessen? (*m.*)

   (e) Wie ist Ihr......... Name, bitte? (*m.*)

   (f) Meine Lehrerin hat ihr......... Schulbücher nicht mit. (*pl.*)

   (g) Wo steht Ihr......... Auto? (*n.*)

   (h) Wir arbeiten in unser......... Büro. (*n.*)

   (i) Wo ist euer......... Wohnung? (*f.*)

   (j) Mein......... Lieblingsfächer sind Mathe und Informatik. (*pl.*)

   (k) Wie heißt dein......... Freundin? (*f.*)

   (l) Leider haben wir kein......... Zeit. (*f.*)

   (m) Ihr......... E-Mail war nicht sehr höflich. (*f.*)

   (n) Olaf geht mit sein......... Freund spazieren. (*m.*)

   (o) Adele singt ihr......... besten Hits. (*pl.*)

   (p) Wo habt ihr euer......... Auto stehen lassen? (*n.*)

'Specials'

   (q) Ich habe .... Ahnung. (*I've no idea.*) (*f.*)

   (r) Ich habe .... Lust. (*I don't want to.*) (*f.*)

   (s) Das war .... Fehler. (*That was my mistake.*) (*m.*)

   (t) .... Meinung nach ... (*In my opinion...*) (*f.*)

Adjective endings

Adjectives after the definite article end in either –e or –en.

	m.	**f.**	**n.**	**pl.**
Nominative	der kleine Hund	die kleine Maus	das kleine Haus	die kleinen Kinder
Accusative	den kleinen Hund	die kleine Maus	das kleine Haus	die kleinen Kinder
Dative	dem kleinen Hund	der kleinen Maus	dem kleinen Haus	den kleinen Kindern

1 Fill the gaps with the suggested adjective and its correct ending.

   (a) Die .... Schülerin bekommt gute Noten. (f., intelligent—)

   (b) Wir fahren mit dem .... Bus in die Stadt. (m., nächst—)

   (c) Hast du den .... Vogel gesehen? (m., gelb—)

   (d) Der .... Lehrer ist streng. (m., altmodisch—)

   (e) Ich kaufe dieses .... Kleid. (n., schwarz—)

   (f) Die .... Reihenhäuser sind schön. (pl., neugebaut—)

   (g) Heute gehen wir in den .... Freizeitpark. (m., modern—)

   (h) Wir müssen dieses .... Fahrrad sauber machen. (n., schmutzig—)

   (i) Morgen gehen wir ins .... Einkaufszentrum. (n., neu—)

   (j) Der .... Zug kommt um 1 Uhr an. (m., verspätet—)

Adjectives after the indefinite article have various endings. This also applies to kein, mein, sein, etc.

	m.	**f.**	**n.**	**pl.**
Nominative	ein kleiner Hund	eine kleine Maus	ein kleines Haus	meine kleinen Kinder
Accusative	einen kleinen Hund	eine kleine Maus	ein kleines Haus	meine kleinen Kinder
Dative	einem kleinen Hund	einer kleinen Maus	einem kleinen Haus	meinen kleinen Kindern

2 Fill the gaps with the suggested adjective and its correct ending.

   (a) München ist eine .... Stadt. (f., umweltfreundlich—)

   (b) Ich suche ein .... T-Shirt. (n., preiswert—)

   (c) Marta hat ihre .... Handtasche verloren. (f., modisch—)

   (d) Wir haben unsere .... Hausaufgaben nicht gemacht.
       (pl., schwierig—)

   (e) Ich habe ein .... Bett gekauft. (n., bequem—)

   (f) Das ist ein .... Problem. (n., groß—)

   (g) Das war vielleicht eine .... Stunde! (f., langweilig—)

   (h) Diese .... Leute haben das Spiel verdorben. (pl., idiotisch—)

   (i) Mein Vater hat einen .... Unfall gehabt. (m., schwer—)

   (j) Klaus liebt seine .... Freundin. (f., neu—)

   (k) Wir haben kein .... Obst. (n., frisch—)

   (l) Maria hat einen .... Mantel gekauft. (m., grün—)

Comparisons

> To make comparisons between things, you use the comparative or superlative.
>
> Add *–er* for the comparative, or add *–(e)ste* for the superlative.
>
> Adjective: langsam – langsamer – langsamst- + ending (*slow, slower, slowest*)
>
> Adverb: langsam – langsamer – am langsamsten (*slowly, more slowly, most slowly*)

1 Insert the comparative and superlative forms.

   (a) Mathe ist langweilig, Physik ist .... , aber das .... Fach ist Kunst.

   (b) Oliver läuft schnell, Ali läuft .... , aber Tim läuft am ....

   (c) Berlin ist schön, Paris ist .... , aber Wien ist die .... Stadt.

   (d) Rihanna ist cool, Katy Perry ist .... , aber Taylor Swift ist die .... Sängerin.

   (e) Metallica ist .... als Motörhead. (laut)

   (f) Bremen ist .... als Hamburg. (klein)

   (g) Deine Noten sind schlecht, aber meine sind noch ....

   (h) Ich finde Englisch .... als Französisch, aber Deutsch finde ich am .... (einfach)

   (i) Skifahren ist .... als Radfahren. (schwierig)

   (j) Mein Auto ist .... als dein Auto, aber das Auto meines Vaters ist am .... (billig)

> Some adjectives have small changes to the comparative and superlative forms.

2 Fill in the gaps with the words provided below, then translate the sentences into English.

   beste / länger / höher / besser / größer / jünger / am längsten

   (a) Ich bin .... als du. (jung)

   ....

   (b) Die Alpen sind .... als der Snowdon. (hoch)

   ....

   (c) München ist .... als Bonn. (groß)

   ....

   (d) Meine Haare sind lang, Timos Haare sind .... , aber deine Haare sind ....

   ....

   (e) Fußball ist gut, Handball ist .... , aber Tennis ist das .... Spiel.

   ....

3 Compare your likes and dislikes by using *gern*, *lieber* and *am liebsten*.

   (a) Ich spiele .... Basketball. (*like*)

   (b) Ich esse .... Gemüse als Fleisch. (*prefer*)

   (c) Am .... gehe ich schwimmen. (*like best*)

Personal pronouns

Like *der*, *die* and *das*, pronouns change depending on what case they are in: nominative, accusative or dative.

Nominative	Accusative	Dative
ich	mich	mir
du	dich	dir
er	ihn	ihm
sie	sie	ihr
es	es	ihm
wir	uns	uns
ihr	euch	euch
Sie/sie	Sie/sie	Ihnen/ihnen

1　Use the correct pronoun in the appropriate case.

(a)　Ich liebe .... (*you, familiar*)

(b)　Liebst du ....? (*me*)

(c)　Kommst du mit ....? (*me*)

(d)　Mein Bruder ist nett. Ich mag .... gern. (*him*)

(e)　Ich habe keine Kreditkarte. Ich habe .... verloren. (*it*)

(f)　Ein Geschenk für ....? Danke! (*us*)

(g)　Wir haben .... gestern gesehen. (*you, plural, familiar*)

(h)　Haben .... gut geschlafen? (*you, formal*)

(i)　Die Party ist bei .... (*me*)

(j)　Rolf hatte Hunger. Ich bin mit .... essen gegangen. (*him*)

(k)　Vergiss .... nicht! (*me*)

(l)　Wie heißt ....? (*you, familiar*)

(m)　Wie heißen ....? (*you, formal*)

(n)　Meine Schwester ist krank. Gestern sind wir zu .... gegangen. (*her*)

Certain special phrases use a dative pronoun.

es tut **mir** leid	*I am sorry*
es gefällt **ihm**	*he likes it*
es fällt **mir** schwer	*I find it difficult*
es gelingt **mir**	*I succeed*
es geht **mir** gut	*I'm well*
es tut **ihr** weh	*it hurts her*
das schmeckt **mir**	*that tastes good*
das ist **mir** egal	*it's all the same to me*

2　Fill in the gaps.

(a)　Schwimmen .... mir .... (= *I find it hard*)

(b)　Mmmm, Eis! .... es ....? (= *do you [familiar] like the taste?/ do you like it?*)

(c)　Aua! Das .... weh! (= *it hurts me*)

(d)　Leider .... es .... nicht gut. (= *we aren't well*)

(e)　Wer gewinnt im Fußball? Das .... (= *I don't care*)

(f)　Es .... leid. (= *we are sorry*)

Word order

In German sentences, the **second** item is always the **verb**. In the perfect tense, the part of *haben* or *sein* comes in second position (see below). Here are some present tense examples:

Daniel **fährt** in die Stadt.

Morgen **fährt** Daniel in die Stadt.

1 Rewrite these sentences so that they start with the word or phrases at the beginning of each line.

(a) Die Fernsehsendung beginnt.

Um 6 Uhr ....

(b) Ich fahre mit dem Bus zur Arbeit.

Jeden Tag ....

(c) Meine Eltern sind krank.

Leider ....

(d) Man darf nicht rauchen.

Hier ....

In the perfect tense, the part of *haben* or *sein* comes in second position.

Ich **bin** zum Jugendklub gegangen.

Am Samstag **bin** ich zum Jugendklub gegangen.

2 Now rewrite these sentences.

(a) Wir haben Eis gegessen.

Gestern ....

(b) Timo ist ins Kino gegangen.

Manchmal ....

(c) Ali ist nach Frankreich gefahren.

Letztes Jahr ....

(d) Du hast Pommes gekauft.

Heute Morgen ....

Remember the word order in German: first **time**, then **manner**, then **place**.

| | T | M | P |

Ich spiele <u>jeden Tag</u> <u>mit meinem Bruder</u> <u>im Garten</u>.

3 Write out these sentences in the right order.

(a) jeden Tag / Ich fahre / zur Schule / mit dem Rad

....

(b) am Wochenende / Gehst du / zum Schwimmbad? / mit mir

....

(c) oft / fern / Wir sehen / im Wohnzimmer

....

(d) Tischtennis / Mehmet spielt / im Jugendklub / abends

....

(e) im Büro / Mein Vater arbeitet / fleißig / seit 20 Jahren

....

(f) heute Abend / Willst du / Pizza essen? / im Restaurant / mit mir

....

Conjunctions

> The most common conjunction that introduces a subordinate clause is *weil* (because). It sends the verb to the end.
>
>   Ich gehe oft auf Partys, **weil** sie lustig **sind**.

1 Join these sentences together using *weil*. Write the sentences out.

(a) Claudia will Sportlehrerin werden. Sie ist sportlich.

    ....

(b) Ich kann dich nicht anrufen. Mein Handy funktioniert nicht.

    ....

(c) Wir fahren nach Spanien. Das Wetter ist dort so schön.

    ....

(d) Du darfst nicht im Garten spielen. Es regnet noch.

    ....

(e) Peter hat seine Hausaufgaben nicht gemacht. Er ist faul.

    ....

(f) Ich mag Computerspiele. Sie sind so aufregend.

    ....

> The following conjunctions also send the verb to the end: *als, bevor, bis, da, damit, dass, nachdem, ob, obwohl, während, was, wie, wenn*. In the perfect tense, the part of *haben* or *sein* comes last. In the future tense, it is *werden* that comes at the end.
>
>   Ich habe Golf gespielt, **während** du eingekauft **hast**.

2 Join the sentences together using the conjunction in brackets. Write the sentences out.

(a) Du kannst abwaschen. Ich koche. (während)

    ....

(b) Wir kaufen oft ein. Wir sind in der Stadt. (wenn)

    ....

(c) Ich kann nicht zur Party kommen. Ich werde arbeiten. (da)

    ....

(d) Lasst uns früh aufstehen. Wir können wandern. (damit)

    ....

(e) Meine Eltern waren böse. Ich bin nicht spät nach Hause gekommen. (obwohl)

    ....

(f) Ich habe es nicht gewusst. Du bist krank. (dass)

    ....

(g) Papa hat geraucht. Er war jung. (als)

    ....

(h) Ich weiß nicht. Man repariert einen Computer. (wie)

    ....

(i) Wir können schwimmen gehen. Das Wetter ist gut. (wenn)

    ....

(j) Wir müssen warten. Es regnet nicht mehr. (bis)

    ....

More on word order

> *um … zu* means 'in order to'. It needs an infinitive at the end of the clause.
>
>   Wir gehen in den Park, **um** Tennis **zu** spielen.

1 Combine these sentences with *um … zu*. Write the sentences out.

(a) Wir fahren in die Stadt. Wir kaufen Lebensmittel.

....

(b) Viele Leute spielen Tennis. Sie werden fit.

....

(c) Boris spart Geld. Er kauft ein Motorrad.

....

(d) Meine Schwester geht zur Abendschule. Sie lernt Französisch.

....

(e) Ich bin gestern zum Imbiss gegangen. Ich esse gern Pommes.

....

> There are some other expressions which use *zu* in the same way.

2 Complete the sentences.

(a) Das Orchester beginnt .... (*to play*)

(b) Wir hoffen, ... (*to learn Spanish*)

(c) Oliver versucht, ... (*to play guitar*)

> Relative pronouns, *der*, *die* or *das* (expressing 'who' or 'that' or 'which') send the verb to the end of the clause.
>
>   das Mädchen, **das** krank **ist**   *the girl who is ill*

3 Translate these expressions into German. You will find the expressions jumbled up in the box below.

(a) the girl who plays tennis

....

(b) the boy who sings well

....

(c) the man who speaks German

....

(d) the house (*n.*) that is old

....

(e) the subject (*n.*) that is hard

....

(f) the car (*n.*) that is broken

....

(g) the cup (*f.*) that is full

....

das Auto,	das Fach,	der Deutsch spricht	das alt ist
der Junge,	das Mädchen,	das kaputt ist	das schwer ist
der Mann,	das Haus,	der gut singt	die voll ist
die Tasse,			das Tennis spielt

The present tense

Verb endings in the present tense change according to who or what is doing the action.

ich	mach**e**	*I do/make*
du	mach**st**	*you do/make*
er/sie/es/man	mach**t**	*he/she/it/one does/makes*
wir	mach**en**	*we do/make*
ihr	mach**t**	*you do/make*
Sie/sie	mach**en**	*you/they do/make*

1   Write in the correct form of the verb indicated. These verbs are all regular in the present tense.

(a) wir .... (*go*)

(b) er .... (*find*)

(c) sie *(singular)* .... (*sing*)

(d) ich .... (*play*)

(e) ihr .... (*do*)

(f) du .... (*say*)

(g) es .... (*come*)

(h) sie *(plural)* .... (*swim*)

(i) ich .... (*hear*)

(j) wir .... (*drink*)

Some verbs have a vowel change in the *du* and *er/sie/es/man* forms of the present tense.

2   Insert the correct form of the present tense, then translate the sentences into English.

schläfst / fahrt / esst / isst / gibt / spricht / sprecht / nimmst / liest / lest / fährt / hilfst

(a) Was .... du? (lesen)

....

(b) .... du? (schlafen)

....

(c) Annabelle .... nicht gern Fleisch. (essen)

....

(d) Kerstin .... gut Englisch. (sprechen)

....

(e) .... du Zucker? (nehmen)

....

(f) Ben .... bald nach Berlin. (fahren)

....

(g) .... du mir, bitte? (helfen)

....

(h) Mein Onkel .... mir 20 Euro. (geben)

....

3   Circle any irregular present tense verbs in this list.

er spricht / du siehst / sie macht / es liegt / ich sage / sie fährt / du kommst / er liest

Separable and reflexive verbs

Separable verbs have two parts: a prefix and the main verb. In a sentence, the prefix goes to the end.

einsteigen (*to get in*): Ich **steige** (*verb*) in das Taxi **ein** (*prefix*).

1 Fill in the two gaps in these sentences.

(a) Wir .... bald .... (ankommen)

(b) Er .... um 7 Uhr .... (abfahren)

(c) Wir .... oft Filme .... (herunterladen)

(d) Wie oft .... du .... ? (fernsehen)

(e) Wo .... man .... ? (aussteigen)

(f) Ich .... die Tür .... (zumachen)

Separable verbs form the past participle as one word with the *ge-* in the middle: *ausgestiegen.*

2 Put the above sentences into the perfect tense.

(a) ....

(b) ....

(c) ....

(d) ....

(e) ....

(f) ....

Reflexive verbs are always used with a reflexive pronoun (*mich, dich, sich,* etc.).

ich freue **mich**	wir freuen **uns**
du freust **dich**	ihr freut **euch**
er/sie/es/man freut **sich**	Sie/sie freuen **sich**

Ich amüsiere **mich** gut am Computer.

3 Fill in the correct reflexive pronoun, then translate the sentences into English.

(a) Ich interessiere .... für Geschichte.

....

(b) Sara freut .... auf die Ferien.

....

(c) Erinnerst du .... an mich?

....

(d) Wir langweilen .... in der Schule.

....

(e) Ich habe .... noch nicht entschieden.

....

(f) Tina hat .... heute nicht geschminkt.

....

(g) Habt ihr .... gut amüsiert?

....

(h) Unser Haus befindet .... in der Nähe vom Bahnhof.

....

Commands

When telling someone what to do using the *Sie* (polite) form, swap the present tense round so the verb comes before the pronoun.

  Stehen Sie auf!

1 Using the *Sie* form, tell someone…

  (a) …not to park here. (parken)

....

  (b) …not to talk so loudly. (sprechen)

....

  (c) …to get off here. (aussteigen)

....

  (d) …not to drive so fast. (fahren)

....

  (e) …to come in. (hereinkommen)

....

  (f) …to go straight on. (gehen)

....

  (g) …to come back soon. (wiederkommen)

....

  (h) …to give you 10 euros. (geben)

....

When telling someone what to do using the *du* (familiar) form, use the present tense *du* form minus the –*st* ending.

  Steh auf!

2 Tell a friend…

  (a) …to get up. (aufstehen)

....

  (b) …to write soon. (schreiben)

....

  (c) …to come here. (herkommen)

....

  (d) …to take two. (nehmen)

....

  (e) …to bring you the ball. (bringen)

....

  (f) …to stop. (aufhören)

....

  (g) …to behave. (sich benehmen)

....

  (h) …to sit down. (sich setzen)

....

Present tense modals

Modal verbs (*können, müssen, wollen, dürfen, sollen, mögen*) can't be used on their own. They need to be used with the infinitive of another verb at the end of the sentence.

1 Write in the modal verb and the infinitive. Use words from the box below.

(a) Ich .... nicht schnell .... (*can't run*)

(b) Wir .... bald Kaffee .... (*must buy*)

(c) Kinder .... keinen Alkohol .... (*shouldn't drink*)

(d) Claudia .... nicht .... (*doesn't like to swim*)

(e) Schüler .... hier nicht .... (*aren't allowed to sit*)

(f) Wir .... Pommes .... (*want to eat*)

(g) Hier .... man .... (*is allowed to park*)

(h) Meine Eltern .... eine neue Wohnung ....
    (*want to rent*)

(i) Du .... gut Fußball .... (*can play*)

(j) Sie (*polite*) .... höflich .... (*should be*)

darf / dürfen / kann / kannst / müssen / soll / sollten / mag / wollen / wollen
essen / mieten / kaufen / laufen / parken / sein / sitzen / spielen / trinken / schwimmen

2 Make these sentences into modal sentences, using the verbs provided.

Man trinkt nicht zu viel. (sollen) ⟶ Man **soll** nicht zu viel **trinken**.

(a) Im Kino raucht man nicht. (dürfen)

....

(b) Wir gehen zur Bowlingbahn. (mögen)

....

(c) Meine Freunde bleiben zu Hause. (wollen)

....

(d) Ihr esst weniger. (müssen)

....

(e) Man isst nicht viel Zucker. (sollen)

....

(f) Ergül spielt gut Gitarre. (können)

....

(g) Hilfst du mir bei meinen Hausaufgaben? (können)

....

(h) Man spielt hier nie. (dürfen)

....

(i) Wir fahren mit der Straßenbahn. (müssen)

....

(j) Ich esse meinen Salat nicht. (wollen)

....

Imperfect modals

To use modals in the past, take the imperfect of the modal verb. The infinitive is sent to the end of the sentence.

	ich / er	**I / he**
müssen	musste	*had to*
wollen	wollte	*wanted to*
dürfen	durfte	*was allowed to*
sollen	sollte	*was supposed to*
mögen	mochte	*liked*
können	konnte	*was able to/could*

1 Put these present modals into the imperfect.

(a) ich will ....

(b) wir müssen ....

(c) sie können ....

(d) sie darf ....

(e) man soll ....

(f) er mag ....

(g) wir wollen ....

(h) Jutta kann ....

2 Put these modal sentences into the imperfect.

Er kann gut singen. ⟶ Er **konnte** gut singen.

(a) Du sollst gesund essen.

....

(b) Wir müssen nach Hause gehen.

....

(c) Ella mag nicht Musik hören.

....

(d) Wir wollen im Internet surfen.

....

(e) Ich kann gut Tischtennis spielen.

....

(f) Ihr dürft spät ins Bett gehen.

....

Möchte (would like to) and *könnte* (could) are two other very useful forms. They also send the infinitive to the end.

3 Translate these sentences.

Would you like to come along? ⟶ Möchtest du mitkommen?

(a) Would you (*Sie*) like to play tennis?

....

(b) We could go shopping.

....

(c) I'd like to eat an ice cream.

....

(d) Could you (*du*) help me?

....

The perfect tense 1

Use the perfect tense to talk about something you have done in the past.

Form the perfect tense by using the verb *haben* plus the past participle at the end of the sentence.

Wir **haben** zu viel **gegessen**.

1 Unjumble these perfect tense sentences.

(a) Wir gespielt haben Minigolf.

....

(b) gekauft ihr neue Habt Schuhe?

....

(c) besucht du deine Hast Oma?

....

(d) Was gesagt hat er?

....

(e) habe Ich gelernt Spanisch.

....

(f) Hast gelesen du diese Zeitung?

....

(g) ein Geschenk Dennis gegeben hat mir.

....

(h) gesehen einen haben tollen Wir Film.

....

Some verbs of movement use *sein* instead of *haben* to form the perfect tense.

2 Insert the correct form of *sein* and a past participle.

(a) Wohin .... du ....? (fahren)

(b) Wir .... nach Mallorca .... (fahren)

(c) Ich .... zu Hause .... (bleiben)

(d) Usain Bolt .... schnell .... (laufen)

(e) Meine Mutter .... nach Amerika .... (fliegen)

(f) Der Zug .... (abfahren)

3 Circle the correct verb: *haben* or *sein*?

(a) Abdul hat / ist 12 Stunden geschlafen.

(b) Wir haben / sind unsere Hausaufgaben gemacht.

(c) Wohin hast / bist du gefahren?

(d) Ich habe / bin spät nach Hause gekommen.

(e) Habt / Seid ihr Britta gesehen?

The perfect tense 2

Many past participles are irregular and just have to be learned.

1 What are the past participles of these common verbs?

(a) schwimmen ....   (i) sprechen ....

(b) sein   ....   (j) treffen   ....

(c) schließen   ....   (k) werden   ....

(d) essen   ....   (l) trinken   ....

(e) stehen   ....   (m) nehmen   ....

(f) sitzen   ....   (n) singen   ....

(g) schreiben   ....   (o) haben   ....

(h) sterben   ....

2 Now put these sentences into the perfect tense.

Wir sehen einen Film. ⟶ Wir **haben** einen Film **gesehen**.

(a) Wir schreiben eine E-Mail.

....

(b) Wir treffen uns um 6 Uhr.

....

(c) Niemand stirbt.

....

(d) Nimmst du mein Handy?

....

(e) Ich esse eine Bratwurst.

....

(f) Er trinkt ein Glas Cola.

....

(g) Wir schwimmen im Meer.

....

(h) Marita spricht Italienisch.

....

• Separable verbs add the *ge* between the prefix and the verb.

    einladen ⟶ ein**ge**laden

• Verbs starting *be-*, *emp-*, *er-* or *ver-* don't add *ge* to the past participle.

    verstehen ⟶ verstanden

---

3 Work out the past participles of these verbs.

(a) vergessen ....   (e) besuchen   ....

(b) ankommen   ....   (f) herunterladen ....

(c) empfehlen ....   (g) abfahren   ....

(d) verlieren ....   (h) aussteigen   ....

The imperfect tense

To form the imperfect (simple past) of regular verbs, take the *–en* off the infinitive, then add *t* and the ending.

ich hör**te**	*I heard/was hearing*
du hör**test**	*you heard/were hearing*
er/sie/es/man hör**te**	*he/she/it/one heard/was hearing*
wir hör**ten**	*we heard/were hearing*
ihr hör**tet**	*you heard/were hearing*
Sie/sie hör**ten**	*you/they heard/were hearing*

1 Put these sentences into the imperfect.

Wir hören Musik. ⟶ Wir **hörten** Musik.

(a) Ich spiele am Computer.

....

(b) Was sagst du?

....

(c) Nina kauft Chips.

....

(d) Die Schüler lernen Englisch.

....

(e) Es schneit im Winter.

....

(f) Peter lacht laut.

....

Haben and *sein* have an irregular imperfect form: *hatte* and *war*, plus the appropriate endings.

2 Fill in the gaps with the imperfect tense of *sein* or *haben*.

(a) Es .... gestern kalt.

(b) Wir .... auf der Party viel Spaß.

(c) Paul .... im Krankenhaus.

(d) Meine Eltern .... drei Kinder.

(e) Ich .... gestern im Imbiss.

(f) .... du Angst?

There are some irregular imperfect tense verbs which have to be learned.

3 Write **P** if the verb is in the present tense and **I** if it is in the imperfect.

(a) Es gab viel zu essen. ....   (g) Sie kamen um 6 Uhr an. ....

(b) Wir sitzen im Kino. ....   (h) Wie findest du das? ....

(c) Es tut mir leid! ....   (i) Aua! Das tat weh! ....

(d) Ich fahre nach Berlin. ....   (j) Ich fand es gut. ....

(e) Er kommt früh an. ....   (k) Es gibt nicht viel zu tun. ....

(f) Er saß im Wohnzimmer. ....   (l) Klaus fuhr zu schnell. ....

The future tense

It is quite common to use the present tense to indicate the future.

Ich komme bald nach Hause.   *I'm coming home soon.*

1   Use the present tense to indicate the future. Put the future expression straight after the verb.

Wir (gehen) einkaufen (morgen). ⟶ Wir gehen morgen einkaufen.

(a) Susi (gehen) auf die Uni (nächstes Jahr).

....

(b) Wir (fahren) nach Ibiza (im Sommer).

....

(c) Er (kommen) zu uns (übermorgen).

....

(d) Ich (bleiben) zu Hause (heute Abend).

....

(e) (Bringen) du deine Schwester mit (am Wochenende)?

....

To form the actual future tense, use the present tense of **werden** with the infinitive at the end of the sentence.

ich werde	wir werden
du wirst	ihr werdet
er/sie/es/man wird	Sie/sie werden

2   Insert the correct form of *werden* and the appropriate infinitive from the box below.

Olaf **wird** Cola **trinken**.

(a) Ich .... um 6 Uhr .... (*leave*)

(b) .... du am Wochenende Musik ....? (*listen*)

(c) .... ihr Pizza ....? (*eat*)

(d) Wir .... die Prüfung .... (*pass*)

(e) Nächstes Jahr .... wir nach Afrika .... (*travel*)

(f) Daniel .... einen Film .... (*download*)

(g) Ich .... ein Problem mit meinem Laptop .... (*have*)

(h) Bayern München .... das Spiel .... (*win*)

(i) Meine Freunde .... um 9 Uhr .... (*arrive*)

(j) Meine Schwester .... im August .... (*get married*)

heiraten / reisen / hören / essen / herunterladen / gewinnen / haben / ankommen / abfahren / bestehen

3   Write three sentences about things you will do in the future.

(a) ....

....

(b) ....

....

(c) ....

....

The conditional

To form the conditional, use part of *würde* plus the infinitive at the end.

ich würde	wir würden
du würdest	ihr würdet
er/sie/es/man würde	Sie/sie würden

1 Fill in the gaps with the correct part of *würde*.

   (a) Wenn wir Zeit hätten, ... wir einkaufen gehen.

   (b) Wenn meine Eltern Geld hätten, ... sie ein Auto kaufen.

   (c) Wenn ich Kinder hätte, ... ich sie lieben.

   (d) Wenn Tanja nicht krank wäre, ... sie Skateboard fahren.

   (e) Wenn du fleißiger wärst, ... du deine Prüfung bestehen.

   (f) Wenn das Wetter besser wäre, ... wir Sport treiben.

The conditional of *haben* is *hätte*, with the appropriate endings. The conditional of *sein* is *wäre*, with the appropriate endings.

2 Fill in the gaps with the correct form of *hätte* or *wäre*.

   (a) Wenn ich Krankenschwester ...., würde ich mich freuen.

   (b) Wenn er Klempner ...., würde er viel verdienen.

   (c) Wenn wir in einer Fabrik arbeiten würden, ... wir müde.

   (d) Wenn wir Glasflaschen ...., würden wir sie recyceln.

   (e) Wenn ich Hunger ...., würde ich eine Bratwurst essen.

   (f) Wenn Manya und Timo Talent ...., würden sie in einer Band spielen.

ich möchte	*I would like*
ich hätte gern	*I would like to have*

3 Write three sentences about things you'd like to do. Start with *Ich möchte…*

   (a) ....

   ....

   (b) ....

   ....

   (c) ....

   ....

4 Write three sentences about things you'd like to have. Start with *Ich hätte gern…*

   (a) ....

   ....

   (b) ....

   ....

   (c) ....

   ....

The pluperfect tense

To form the pluperfect, (i.e. what **had** happened), use the imperfect form of *haben* or *sein* plus the past participle at the end.

ich hatte   wir hatten
du hattest   ihr hattet
er/sie/es/man hatte   Sie/sie hatten

Ich **hatte** mein Buch **vergessen**.   *I had forgotten my book.*

1   Insert the correct part of *haben* or *sein*, plus a past participle, to make these sentences pluperfect.

(a) Wir .... Kaffee und Kuchen .... (*had ordered*)

(b) .... du Spaß ....? (*had had*)

(c) Ich .... eine neue Stelle .... (*had got*)

(d) Wir .... unsere Freunde .... (*had invited*)

(e) Als ich nach Hause .... (*had come*), habe ich gegessen.

(f) Kagan .... zur Bäckerei .... (*had gone*)

(g) Sie (*plural*) .... zu Hause .... (*had stayed*)

(h) Ich .... mit dem Auto nach Frankfurt .... (*had driven*)

2   Write out these perfect-tense sentences in the pluperfect. You only need to change the part of *haben* or *sein*.

(a) Es ist nicht passiert.

     ....

(b) Ich habe dir eine E-Mail geschickt.

     ....

(c) Hast du dich nicht geschminkt?

     ....

(d) Ich bin sehr früh eingeschlafen.

     ....

(e) Opa ist noch nie nach London gefahren.

     ....

(f) Bist du zur Haltestelle gegangen?

     ....

(g) Wir haben unseren Müll zur Mülldeponie gebracht.

     ....

(h) Er hat zwei Computerspiele heruntergeladen.

     ....

(i) Die Fabrik ist sehr laut gewesen.

     ....

(j) Fatima hat Abitur gemacht.

     ....

Questions

To ask a simple question, just swap the pronoun (or name) and the verb around.

Du bist krank. ⟶ Bist du krank?

1 Make these statements into questions.

(a) Kevin spielt oft am Computer.

....

(b) Du hast dein Handy verloren.

....

(c) Wir wollen Volleyball spielen.

....

(d) Hakan studiert Informatik.

....

(e) Ihr geht morgen zum Sportzentrum.

....

2 Ask the questions to which these are the answers.

Ja, ich habe Chips gekauft. ⟶ Hast du Chips gekauft?

(a) Nein, ich bin nicht zum Supermarkt gefahren.

....

(b) Ja, Ayse wird Chemie studieren.

....

(c) Nein, mein Auto ist nicht kaputt.

....

(d) Ja, ich esse gern Bratwurst mit Pommes.

....

(e) Ja, morgen wird es regnen.

....

You have to learn the German question words.

3 Draw lines to link the English and German question words.

who?	wessen?
what?	wie viele?
how?	warum?
when?	was für?
why?	wer?
where?	mit wem?
how many?	wie?
what kind of?	wann?
whose?	was?
who with?	wo?

4 Write three questions you could ask during a role play about visiting a town.

(a) ....

(b) ....

(c) ....

Time markers

Time markers are useful words for showing when something happens, did happen or will happen.

1 Write down the tense (present, past or future) that these time markers indicate.

(a) gestern ....   (f) normalerweise ....

(b) früher ....   (g) vor zwei Wochen ....

(c) bald ....   (h) morgen ....

(d) letzte Woche ....   (i) nächste Woche ....

(e) heute ....   (j) jetzt ....

2 Draw lines to link the English and German expressions.

1 manchmal   A *immediately*

2 neulich   B *on time*

3 sofort   C *sometimes*

4 täglich   D *in the future*

5 rechtzeitig   E *recently*

6 in Zukunft   F *every day*

3 Rewrite these sentences using the time expressions provided. Put the time expression first and the verb second.

Wir fahren nach Bremen. (morgen) ⟶ Morgen fahren wir nach Bremen.

(a) Ich werde mein Betriebspraktikum machen. (nächste Woche)

....

....

(b) Ulli sieht fern. (heute Abend)

....

....

(c) Man wird Strom sparen. (in Zukunft)

....

....

(d) Du wirst einen Unfall haben. (bald)

....

....

(e) Wir treffen uns mit unseren Freunden. (manchmal)

....

....

(f) Ich war bei meinem Onkel. (neulich)

....

....

(g) Metin hat sein Betriebspraktikum begonnen. (vorgestern)

....

....

(h) Ich gehe zur Bäckerei. (jeden Tag)

....

....

Numbers

Revise the numbers 1–1000. You need to be completely confident in using numbers.

1 Write the German numbers in figures.

(a) vierhunderteinundzwanzig ....

(b) tausendsechshundertvierundvierzig ....

(c) achtundsechzig ....

(d) dreihunderteins ....

(e) siebenundneunzig ....

(f) hundertfünf ....

(g) siebzehn ....

(h) sechshundertdreiundfünfzig ....

2 Choose from the list on the right the correct cardinal number to fill each gap by drawing a linking line.

(a) Es ist .... nach .... (20, 9)   sieben

(b) Ausverkauf! .... Prozent Rabatt! (15)   zwölf

(c) Es ist .... Grad. (13)   dreißig

(d) Ich habe .... Euro gewonnen. (650)   fünfzehn

(e) Der Zug kommt um .... Minuten vor .... an. (12, 7) dreizehn

(f) Es gibt .... Schüler in meiner Klasse. (30)   sechshundertfünfzig

neun

zwanzig

Revise the ordinal numbers. Note that they take adjectival endings.

1st	erste	*20th*	zwanzigste
2nd	zweite	*21st*	einundzwanzigste
3rd	dritte	*30th*	dreißigste
4th	vierte	*31st*	einunddreißigste
5th	fünfte		
6th	sechste		
7th	siebte		

3 Write the dates in numbers.

der einunddreißigste Mai ⟶ 31.5.

(a) der zwölfte März ....

(b) der dreizehnte Juli ....

(c) der achtundzwanzigste Dezember ....

(d) der erste April ....

(e) der dritte Januar ....

(f) der siebzehnte Juni ....

4 Write in the ordinal numbers.

(a) Mein Geburtstag ist am .... November. (*1st*)

(b) Saschas Geburtstag ist am .... September. (*7th*)

(c) Das Konzert findet am .... Mai statt. (*12th*)

(d) Die Ferien beginnen am .... Juli. (*2nd*)

Practice test: Listening 1

AQA publishes official sample assessment material on its website. These practice tests have been written to help you practise what you have learned across the four skills, and may not be representative of a real exam paper.

Shopping for clothes

1 The department store's radio is asking people about their purchases today.

What are they buying?

Write the correct letter in the box.

(a)

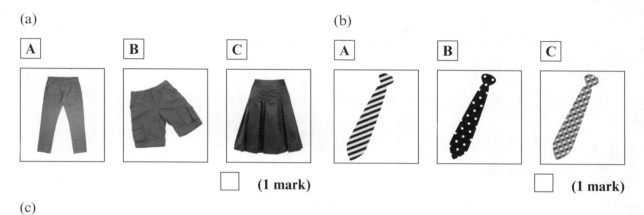

| A | B | C |

☐ **(1 mark)**

(b)

| A | B | C |

☐ **(1 mark)**

(c)

| A | B | C |

☐ **(1 mark)**

Work experience

2 Your German exchange partner Luka is talking about his sister Mia and her work experience placement.

Where does Mia want to do work experience this year and what is Luka's opinion of this?

Complete the table **in English.**

Mia's work placement wish	Luka's opinion

(2 marks)

Practice test: Listening 2

Listen to the recording

Friends

1 Your Swiss friend Lara calls you and tells you about her group of friends.

Answer all the questions **in English**.

(a) When did Oli make his friends laugh?

.... **(1 mark)**

(b) Why does Oli not join in with the group these days?

.... **(1 mark)**

(c) What did Emma organise for the group recently?

.... **(1 mark)**

(d) What does Lara think Emma might be one day?

.... **(1 mark)**

Listen to the recording

Urlaubspläne

2 Du hörst diesen Bericht vom Reisebüro.

Beantworte die beiden Teile der Frage.

Schreib den richtigen Buchstaben in das Kästchen.

(a) Was werden viele Kunden dieses Jahr machen?

A	Zu Hause bleiben
B	Ins Ausland fahren
C	Eine Ferienwohnung mieten

☐ **(1 mark)**

(b) Warum liegt Spanien an erster Stelle? Beantworte die Frage **auf Deutsch**.

.... **(1 mark)**

Practice test: Listening 3

At school

Listen to the
recording

1   You hear an interview on the school radio with Melina talking about her classmates.

Answer all the questions **in English**.

(a) Give **one** example of how Ivan showed he was shy last year.

....   **(1 mark)**

(b) How has Melina's attitude to him changed?

....   **(1 mark)**

(c) What was Olivia's behaviour like in class last year? Give **two** examples.

....

....   **(2 marks)**

(d) What reason is given for Olivia becoming friendlier?

....   **(1 mark)**

Advantages of sport

Listen to the
recording

2   You hear a report about sport and young people on Swiss radio.

Which **three** statements are true?

Write the correct letters in the boxes.

A	Physical activity is popular with young people.
B	A sedentary lifestyle is more popular than an active one.
C	Machines reduce the amount of exercise people take.
D	Sport does not contribute to mental well-being.
E	Team sport is not popular with adults.
F	Sport could make people happier.

☐ ☐ ☐   **(3 marks)**

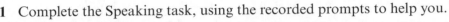

Practice test: Speaking 1

1   Complete the Speaking task, using the recorded prompts to help you.

Listen to the recording

Topic: Transport and travel

Instructions to candidates:

Your teacher will play the part of the ticket office employee and will speak first.

You should address the ticket office employee as *Sie*.

When you see this – ! – you will have to respond to something you have not prepared.

When you see this – ? – you will have to ask a question.

> Prepare your answer using the prompts. Then listen to the recording and speak your answer aloud in the pauses.

Task

Sie sind am Bahnhof und wollen eine Zugfahrkarte kaufen. Sie sprechen mit dem/der Angestellten.

1 Fahrt – Tag

2 Fahrt – Uhrzeit

3 !

4 Grund für Fahrt (**ein** Detail)

5 ? Preis

> There is a full sample dialogue on page 132 of the Answers section to give you more ideas.

2   Complete the Speaking task, using the recorded prompts to help you.

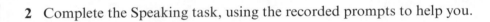

Listen to the recording

Topic: Technology

Instructions to candidates:

Your teacher will play the part of your exchange partner and will speak first.

You should address your partner as *du*.

When you see this – ! – you will have to respond to something you have not prepared.

When you see this – ? – you will have to ask a question

> Prepare your answer using the prompts. Then listen to the recording and speak your answer aloud in the pauses.

Task

Du sprichst mit deinem Austauschpartner/deiner Austauschpartnerin über Computer.

1 Online-Aktivitäten – gestern (**eine** Aktivität)

2 Deine Meinung über Computerspiele (**ein** Detail)

3 !

4 Computer – wie oft

5 ? Online-Pläne – heute Abend

> There is a full sample dialogue in the Answers section to give you more ideas.

Practice test: Speaking 2

1   Complete the picture-based task.

Topic: The environment

- Look at the photo during the preparation period.
- Make any notes you wish on a piece of paper.
- Your teacher will then ask you questions about the photo and about topics related to **the environment**.
  Listen to the audio tracks of the teacher's parts and speak your answers in the pauses.

> When you have prepared your answer, listen to the sample dialogue and read the transcript on pages 132–133 of the Answers section for ideas on what you could include.

- Was gibt es auf dem Foto?
- Wie kann man die Umwelt schützen?
- Wie umweltfreundlich warst du letzte Woche?
- ! (Wie bist du im Urlaub umweltfreundlich?)
- ! (Was macht deine Familie, um der Umwelt zu helfen?)

> Decide whether to try the Foundation or Higher questions – or for extra practice, do both!

- Was gibt es auf dem Foto?
- Wie wichtig ist dir Umweltschutz?
- Wie möchtest du in Zukunft der Umwelt helfen ?
- ! (Ist es wichtiger, Tiere oder Pflanzen zu schützen?)
- ! (Möchtest du für eine Umweltorganisation arbeiten? Warum (nicht)?)

> Remember that these are your two unprepared questions on the photo.

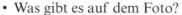

SPEAKING
TRACK 70
Listen to the recording

SPEAKING
TRACK 71
Listen to the recording

Practice test: Reading 1

School

1 Read these profiles of four German teenagers on the class 10 website.

Write the first letter of the correct name in the box.

Write **L** for **Lena**.

Write **R** for **Ralf**.

Write **H** for **Hanna**.

Write **F** for **Frank**.

Lena	Ich bin sehr lustig, aber ziemlich blöd. Ich bin nie schlecht gelaunt und ich habe viele Freunde in der Klasse.
Ralf	Ich bin sehr intelligent, aber ich kann in der Klasse schüchtern sein. Ich spreche nicht gern mit den Lehrern und ich bin oft ängstlich.
Hanna	Ich bin fleißig und mache immer meine Hausaufgaben. In der Pause gehe ich oft in die Bibliothek. Ich lese dort gern.
Frank	Ich bin musikalisch und lade gern Lieder aus dem Internet herunter. Ich spiele Gitarre und singe die ganze Zeit.

(a) Who enjoys reading? ☐   **(1 mark)**

(b) Who is very sociable? ☐   **(1 mark)**

(c) Who enjoys musical hobbies? ☐   **(1 mark)**

Environment

2 Translate this description **into English**.

Meine Mutter spart immer Energie. Zu Hause tragen wir alle warme Pullis. Das ist nervig, weil ich lieber T-Shirts trage. Letzten Mittwoch habe ich den Müll nicht getrennt. Nächste Woche werde ich das jeden Tag machen.

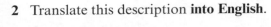

....

....

....

....

....

....

....

....

....   **(9 marks)**

Practice test: Reading 2

Sport

1   You come across this article on a German website while researching sport for a
    school project. Answer the questions **in English**.

> ● ● ●
>
> Teenager heute genießen eine breite Auswahl an Sportarten in der Schule. Das gab es früher nicht.
>
> Viele Jugendliche legen großen Wert darauf, ein gesundes Leben zu führen, und deshalb ist es ihnen wichtig, regelmäßig zu trainieren und Sport zu treiben.
>
> Mehr als 45% aller Jugendlichen gehören entweder einer Sport-AG oder einem Sportverein an. Früher haben solche Gelegenheiten für junge Leute nicht existiert. Man musste warten, bis man älter war.
>
> Hoffentlich geht dieser Trend im Sportbereich so weiter! Dann werden wir wirklich ein aktives Land haben!

(a) What is different for the current generation of teenagers as regards sport?

....   **(1 mark)**

(b) What do young people regard as important? Give **one** detail.

....   **(1 mark)**

(c) How are they unlike their parents as regards sport?

....   **(1 mark)**

(d) Why will it be good if this fashion continues?

....   **(1 mark)**

Part-time work

2   You are thinking of a career in languages and find this profile in a magazine.

Write **T** if the statement is **true**.   Write **NT** if the information is **not in the text**.
Write **F** if the statement is **false**.

> Thomas studiert Fremdsprachen an der Uni. Er muss aber immer einen Nebenjob machen, weil er Geld braucht. Früher hat er am Wochenende und in den Ferien in einem Freizeitzentrum gearbeitet, was ihm besonders gut gefallen hat. Leider hat das Zentrum einen neuen Chef, der keine Studenten im Team haben will.
>
> Thomas musste sich einen anderen Job suchen, um Geld zu verdienen, und er hat sich in mehreren Geschäften in der Stadt beworben. Aber alles ohne Erfolg.
>
> In den Sommerferien wird Thomas jetzt als Küchenhilfe in einem Schnellimbiss in der Stadtmitte arbeiten. Er war sehr froh, als er den Job bekommen hat, weil die Arbeitsstunden ihm gut passen, obwohl das Gehalt enttäuschend niedrig ist.

(a) Thomas learns languages
     at school.   ☐ **(1 mark)**

(b) He now enjoys working.   ☐ **(1 mark)**

(c) He worked in a sports
     centre.   ☐ **(1 mark)**

(d) Thomas lost his job.   ☐ **(1 mark)**

(e) Thomas could not find a
     job in town.   ☐ **(1 mark)**

(f) The snack bar is very
     popular.   ☐ **(1 mark)**

(g) Thomas is looking forward
     to the job.   ☐ **(1 mark)**

(h) He will work five days
     a week.   ☐ **(1 mark)**

Practice test: Reading 3

Die unendliche Geschichte **by Michael Ende**

1 Read the extract from the text.

While fleeing from his schoolmates, Bastian seeks refuge in a shop.

> »Ich heiße Bastian«, sagte der Junge, »Bastian Balthasar Bux.«
>
> »Ziemlich kurioser Name«, knurrte der Mann, »mit diesen drei B's. Na ja, dafür kannst du nichts, du hast dir den Namen ja nicht selbst gegeben. Ich heiße Karl Konrad Koreander.«
>
> »Das sind drei K's«, sagte der Junge ernst.
>
> »Hm«, brummte der Alte, »stimmt! Na ja, ist ja auch ganz gleich, wie wir heißen, da wir uns ja doch nicht wiedersehen. Jetzt möchte ich nur noch eins wissen, nämlich wieso du vorhin mit solchem Krach in meinen Laden eingebrochen bist. … Ich hatte den Eindruck, dass du auf der Flucht wärst.«
>
> Bastian nickte. Sein rundes Gesicht wurde plötzlich noch blasser und seine Augen noch etwas größer.
>
> »Wahrscheinlich hast du eine Ladenkasse ausgeraubt. … Ist die Polizei hinter dir her, mein Kind?«
>
> Bastian schüttelte den Kopf.

Which **four** statements are true?

Write the correct letters in the boxes.

A	Bastian and the old man have something in common.
B	Bastian is very relaxed.
C	Bastian crept into the old man's shop earlier.
D	Bastian drew attention to himself as he entered the shop.
E	Bastian is confident.
F	The old man is right to think Bastian is on the run.
G	The old man thinks the police are after Bastian.
H	Bastian agrees with his suggestion.

☐ ☐ ☐ ☐   **(4 marks)**

Practice test: Reading 4

Familie

1 Lies Alis Blog über seine Familie. Beantworte die Fragen **auf Deutsch**.

> ● ● ●
>
> Als Kind hatte ich eine gute Beziehung zu meinem Vater. Seitdem er meine Stiefmutter geheiratet hat, gibt es immer Krach zwischen uns. Sie ist eifersüchtig und mag es nicht, wenn mein Vater mit mir alleine Zeit verbringt.
>
> Ich kenne meine Stiefmutter erst seit vier Jahren und wir verstehen uns gar nicht gut. Letzten Samstag hat sie verlangt, dass ich für meinen Halbbruder babysitten sollte. Mein Halbbruder sieht zwar sehr süß aus, aber er ist total nervig. Deshalb wollte ich nicht babysitten, und außerdem wollte ich zu dieser Zeit mit der Clique ins Kino gehen.
>
> Ich habe immer noch ein sehr gutes Verhältnis zu meiner Schwester, die fünf Jahre älter als ich ist. Vor drei Jahren ist sie aber in eine eigene Wohnung in der Stadtmitte gezogen, weil sie es zu Hause nicht länger aushalten konnte. Ich vermisse sie sehr, weil wir früher über alles geredet haben.

(a) Warum ist Alis Verhältnis zu seinem Vater schlechter geworden?

.... **(1 mark)**

(b) Wie lange kennt Ali seine Stiefmutter?

.... **(1 mark)**

(c) Was hat Ali neulich besonders geärgert?

.... **(1 mark)**

(d) Mit wem kommt Ali am besten aus?

.... **(1 mark)**

(e) Was findet Ali nicht gut an der Situation mit seiner Schwester?

....

.... **(2 marks)**

Translation

2 Translate this description **into English** for a non-German speaker.

> Mein Vater ist Arzt auf dem Land, obwohl er diesen Job nicht mag. Er muss oft nachts arbeiten und kommt dann erschöpft nach Hause. Er würde viel lieber eine andere Stelle haben, wo die Arbeitsstunden kürzer sind. Bevor er Arzt wurde, hatte er einen Teilzeitjob in einem Laden in der Stadtmitte, was ihm sehr gut gefallen hat.

....

....

....

....

....

.... **(9 marks)**

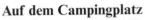
Practice test: Writing 1

Auf dem Campingplatz

1 Du bist auf dem Campingplatz und schickst dieses Foto an deine Freunde in Österreich.

Schreib vier Sätze **auf Deutsch** über das Foto.

.... **(2 marks)**

.... **(2 marks)**

.... **(2 marks)**

.... **(2 marks)**

An der Schule

2 Du schreibst an deinen deutschen Freund über die Schule. Schreib etwas über:

- die Gegend
- die Gebäude
- die Pause
- Events.

Du musst ungefähr **40** Wörter **auf Deutsch** schreiben.

....

....

....

....

.... **(16 marks)**

Had a go ☐   Nearly there ☐   Nailed it! ☐

Practice test: Writing 2

Das Essen

1   Translate the following sentences into **German**.

(a) I like eating chips.

....

....

(b) My brother never eats meat.

....

....

(c) My favourite dessert is cake with chocolate sauce.

....

....

(d) My teacher has to go to hospital.

....

....

(e) At the weekend I drank a bottle of cola.

....

....   **(10 marks)**

Ostern

2   Translate the following passage into **German**.

> Last year at Easter my parents hid lots of eggs in the garden. Every time I found an egg, my brother took it away from me immediately. Next year I won't look for any chocolate, because it is very unhealthy. I would rather spend the money on clothes, which are much more useful.

....

....

....

....

....

....

....

....   **(12 marks)**

Practice test: Writing 3

Mein Zuhause

1   Dein Freund, Sadi, aus der Schweiz hat nach deinem Zuhause gefragt.
   Du schreibst Sadi eine E-Mail über dein Zuhause.

Schreib:

- seit wann du hier wohnst
- was du letztes Wochenende zu Hause gemacht hast
- deine Pläne für die Sommerferien zu Hause
- warum Sadi dich besuchen muss oder nicht.

Du musst ungefähr **90** Wörter **auf Deutsch** schreiben. Schreib etwas über alle
Punkte der Aufgabe.

....

....

....

....

....

....

....

....

....

....

....

....

....

....

....

....

....

.... **(16 marks)**

Practice test: Writing 4

Geld sammeln

1 Du nimmst an einem gesponserten Marathonlauf für ein Wasserprojekt in Afrika teil und schreibst an eine Firma in der Gegend, um Geld für diesen guten Zweck zu sammeln.

- Schreib etwas über das Projekt und wie es den Menschen schon geholfen hat.
- Beschreib, wie du letztes Jahr Geld gesammelt hast und deine Pläne für dieses Jahr.

Du musst ungefähr **150** Wörter **auf Deutsch** schreiben. Schreib etwas über beide Punkte der Aufgabe.

....

....

....

....

....

....

....

....

....

....

....

....

....

....

....

....

....

....

....

....

....

....

....

(32 marks)

Answers

Identity and culture

1. Physical descriptions
1 (a) R, (b) N, (c) M, (d) A, (e) N
2 (a) B, (b) C

2. Character descriptions
1 B, E, G, H
2 (a) Opinion: friendly
Reason: they always give a birthday present
(b) Opinion: mean
Reason: complain when ball lands in their garden

3. Childhood
1 1 B, 2 D, 3 A, 4 E, 5 C

4. Family
1 (a) none
(b) his aunt (Julia)
(c) parents worked late
(d) as strict as his parents / very strict
(e) moved due to parent's work
(f) B
2 (a) Österreich ist ein reiches Land
(b) kein Frühstück / keine festen Schuhe
(c) Familien mit jüngeren Müttern

5. Friends
1 *Sample translations*
(a) Ich liebe meine Freunde/Freundinnen.
(b) Meine Freundin Lottie ist sehr nett/sympathisch.
(c) Sie wohnt neben einem Bahnhof in Berlin.
(d) Wir gehen oft zusammen ins Kino.
(e) Das letzte Mal/Letztes Mal haben wir viel gelacht.
2 *Sample translation*
Ich mache/spiele oft Computerspiele mit meinem Freund Tom. Gestern war ich bei ihm/bei ihm zu Hause, aber sein Bruder war sehr nervig. Tom wird morgen zu mir/zu mir nach Hause kommen. Ich finde es besser, wenn er allein kommt, weil das viel mehr Spaß macht.

6. Peer group
1 1(c), 2(d), 3(b), 4(a)

7. Marriage
1 *Sample translation*
My aunt is marrying her partner. Her new husband is very funny and nice. He is 46 years old and works in an office. We are celebrating first in church and then in a restaurant. At the weekend I bought a new dress.
2 (a) A, (b) C, (c) B, (d) A

8. Partnerships
1 (a) im Wohnzimmer
(b) sein Foto
(c) nette Leute
(d) wir wissen es nicht
2 (a) P, (b) N, (c) P+N, (d) P

9. Social media
1 (a)
(i) 89%
(ii) make contact with people all over the world, communicate in real time
(iii) hide identity behind a screen
(b)
(i) get away from parents
(ii) made new profile
(iii) try to exercise too much control over their children / are not open and honest with them

10. Mobile technology
1 (a) texts
(b) they are better on the big screen
(c) downloads music
(d) strict
(e) making plans with friends/being on her mobile
(f) playing video games
(g) do online shopping
(h) go to the shopping centre

11. Online activities
Sample answer / transcript
Teacher: Was gibt es auf dem Foto?
Student: Das Bild zeigt ein Mädchen, das auf seinem Bett liegt. Sie ist ein Teenager und sie hat lange, glatte Haare. Sie trägt Kopfhörer und sie lächelt, weil sie glücklich ist. Im Vordergrund hat sie einen Computer, aber sie benutzt ihn nicht, weil sie sich auf das Handy konzentriert. Das Mädchen trägt einen hellen Pullover und ihr Schlafzimmer sieht schön aus.
Teacher: Wie findest du Online-Aktivitäten und warum?
Student: Ich finde Online-Aktivitäten super, weil sie so praktisch sind. Wenn ich Probleme mit den Hausaufgaben habe, suche ich die Informationen sofort im Internet. Es ist auch gut, dass man Kinokarten online kaufen kann, weil das Zeit spart. Schlecht daran ist aber, dass man vielleicht zu viel Zeit am Bildschirm verbringt. Es ist sicher gefährlich, wenn man stundenlang am Computer sitzt.
Teacher: Was hast du gestern online gemacht?
Student: Gestern Abend hatte ich keine Hausaufgaben, also habe ich Computerspiele online gespielt. Das hat echt viel Spaß gemacht, weil das Spiel sehr spannend war. Ich habe auch online mit Freunden gechattet und wir haben zusammen etwas für nächstes Wochenende geplant. Ich habe auch eine E-Mail an meinen Austauschpartner geschrieben, um seiner Familie für meinen Besuch bei ihm zu danken.
Teacher: Was willst du heute Abend online machen?
Student: Heute Abend muss ich leider zuerst meine Hausaufgaben am Computer machen. Wir haben zu Hause einen Desktop-PC mit Farbdrucker und hier kann man am besten die Hausaufgaben machen, finde ich. Ich habe auch ein Smartphone und das ist so gut wie ein Computer. Heute Abend will ich Musik herunterladen, soziale Netzwerke besuchen und mit Freunden simsen. Ich habe keine Konsole zu Hause, aber ich kann manche Spiele am Computer spielen. Oder ich kann meinen Freund besuchen und bei ihm spielen. Er hat eine tolle Konsole!
Teacher: Meinst du, Technologie ist unterhaltsam und lustig?
Student: Meiner Meinung nach langweilt man sich nie, wenn man Technologie hat. Man kann sich entweder lustige Videoclips ansehen oder Lieder herunterladen. Mit Technologie kann man jederzeit in Kontakt mit Freunden aus der ganzen Welt bleiben und das ist immer interessant. Ohne Technologie muss das Leben sehr langweilig und einsam sein. Für meine Generation ist es schwer, sich ein Leben ohne Technologie vorzustellen.

12. For and against technology
1 *Sample translation*
I am online every day/daily and I like uploading photos. The biggest advantage for me is that I am always in touch with friends. On the other hand, I would never do internet shopping again. Last year the risk of a virtual life became clear to me, when somebody stole my personal details.
2 (a) B
(b) write emails

13. Everyday life
1 (a) C, (b) B
2 (a) B, (b) B

14. Hobbies
1 (a) piano
   (b) garage
   (c) two from: rock, dance, classical
2 (a) accidents on the slope, dangerous on foggy days
   (b) two from: outside all day, away from town / car fumes / better than being in front of TV / can be by river

15. Interests
1 (a) ein Freizeit-Treffen
   (b) zwei
   (c) um Geld zu verdienen / um einen Beruf zu finden / für die Arbeit
   (d) sie muss Spaß machen / ihr gefallen / Freude machen
   (e) dass dort alle Informationen zum Thema Freizeit präsentiert werden

16. Music
1 Josef: present – listen to music; future – see favourite band
   Jasmin: past – music lesson; present – play guitar
2 (a) er muss erfolgreich sein
   (b) Musik ist in Amerika/den USA sehr beliebt und die Konzerte sind oft ausverkauft; man kann Musik in Amerika verkaufen und Geld verdienen
   (c) Vorbild für junge Musiker zu sein

17. Films
1 (a) former/retired vet
   (b) father and daughter both in it
   (c) waste of money / cheaper to download videos from the internet
   (d) doesn't want to break the law
   (e) subtitles

18. Television
1 (a) B, (b) C, (c) B, (d) B, (e) C
2 B

19. Sport
2 *Sample answer*
   Nächste Woche werden wir im Sportverein ein Sportfest für Jugendliche veranstalten. Das Fest ist kostenlos, aber Besucher müssen im Voraus online einen Platz reservieren. Das Ziel des Festes ist es, Interesse an neuen Sportarten bei unseren jungen Leuten zu wecken. Letztes Jahr war unser Event besonders bei Jugendlichen beliebt, die im Bereich Sport wenig Erfahrung gehabt hatten. Das Fest hat ihnen die ideale Gelegenheit geboten, aufregende Sportarten auszuprobieren. Unsere Trainer waren wie immer freundlich und sie haben alle Fragen beantwortet sowie Rat gegeben. Natürlich wollen wir, wie bei den Olympischen Spielen, dass Jugendliche nach unserem Event weiterhin Sport treiben werden. Im Gegensatz zu vielen Events würden wir nachher einmal pro Monat einen Sporttag organisieren, wo man wieder neue Sportarten ausprobieren könnte. Besonders positiv an unserem Verein ist unser Schwimmbad, wo man verschiedene Wassersportarten machen kann. Bei uns wird jeder Besucher eine große Auswahl an Sportarten haben, was man nicht in jedem Sportverein findet.

20. Food and drink
1 (a) F, (b) T, (c) NT, (d) NT, (e) T, (f) T, (g) F, (h) F

21. Meals
1 (a) im Bad
   (b) 08:15 / Viertel nach acht / acht Uhr fünfzehn
   (c) hübsch
   (d) Toast / Orangenmarmelade
   (e) sentimental / nostalgisch

2 (a) midday meal / lunch
   (b) meat
   (c) Wednesday
   (d) sitting room
   (e) breakfast

22. Eating in a café
1 (a) young people
   (b) tasty / good value
   (c) no dogs allowed
2 (a) food brought to you
   (b) choice not so good / annoying to have to pay first
   (c) you don't have to do it every day
   (d) celebrating a success / birthday
   (e) looks for special offers online

23. Eating in a restaurant
1 Student's own answer
2 Correct order: b, d, a, c

24. Food opinions
1 (a) B, C
   (b) A, C

25. Shopping for clothes
1 *Sample translation*
   Buying clothes can be very tiring, especially if you do not have a typical figure. You can find good value garments / items of clothing at the department store and also at the market. I would suggest to all customers that they always try on the clothes properly in the changing room. In the case that there is a problem, you can change the purchases straight away in order to save time later on.
2 (a) shirt has a hole / on the arm
   (b) it was her son's 18th birthday / they celebrated in the evening
   (c) is going to a barbecue next weekend / wants a new dress to wear

26. Shopping
Sample answer / transcript

Teacher: Was gibt es auf dem Foto?
Student: Das Bild zeigt ein wunderbares Geschäft, wo man schöne Andenken aus der Gegend kaufen kann. Ich denke, dass die Frau im Vordergrund in diesem Geschäft arbeitet. Sie trägt traditionelle Kleidung, weil das den Kunden gefällt. Sie trägt eine Brille und holt ein Souvenir vom Regal. Vielleicht hat jemand das gerade gekauft und sie muss es jetzt als Geschenk einpacken.
Teacher: Kann man in deiner Gegend gut einkaufen?
Student: Leider nicht, denn ich wohne in einem kleinen Dorf auf dem Land. Bei uns gibt es keine Einkaufsmöglichkeiten, außer an der Tankstelle an der Landstraße! Wenn ich etwas kaufen will, fahre ich meistens mit dem Bus in die nächste Stadt und bummle dort durch die Geschäfte. Natürlich kann ich zu jeder Zeit auch online einkaufen, aber ich ziehe es vor, Schuhe und Kleidungsstücke anzuprobieren, bevor ich sie kaufe. Es ist immer ärgerlich, wenn man etwas online bestellt und es dann gleich zurück zum Warenhaus schicken muss, weil es nicht passt.
Teacher: Was hast du in der Grundschule mit deinem Taschengeld gekauft?
Student: Als ich in der Grundschule war, habe ich mein Taschengeld immer für Plastikspielzeug und Schokolade ausgegeben. Eines Tages musste ich zum Zahnarzt gehen und ich war sehr enttäuscht, als ich danach weder Schokolade noch Süßigkeiten mit meinem Geld kaufen durfte. Meine Eltern hatten beides verboten! Zuerst war ich sehr schlecht gelaunt, aber ich habe dann ein neues Hobby entdeckt und habe mein ganzes Geld für Flugzeugmodelle ausgegeben.
Teacher: Was findest du besser: ein Einkaufszentrum am Stadtrand oder Geschäfte in der Stadtmitte?

Listen to the recording

SPEAKING TRACK 73

Student: Ich finde Einkaufszentren unpersönlich und zu groß. Je größer die Auswahl, desto schwieriger wird es, die richtigen Klamotten und Geschenke zu kaufen. Ich finde auch, dass man in diesen Zentren länger Schlange stehen muss, um für die Waren zu bezahlen, und das geht mir auf die Nerven. Die großen Geschäfte auf der Hauptstraße sind ideal, besonders, weil man sie einfach mit den öffentlichen Verkehrsmitteln erreichen kann, was ein großer Vorteil für Jugendliche ist.

Teacher: Wie werden wir in der Zukunft einkaufen?

Student: Ich glaube, dass die Geschäfte nicht sehr anders aussehen werden, aber immer mehr Kunden werden online einkaufen. Auch werden wir wahrscheinlich nie mit Bargeld bezahlen. Stattdessen werden wir mit dem Smartphone oder mit der Karte Einkäufe machen.

27. Customs
1   C, D
2   (a) difference in educational system between Germany and China
    (b) at work
    (c) do a language course / be prepared for chaotic streets/ traffic

28. Greetings
1   (a) C, (b) A, (c) B, (d) A
2   (a) Christmas
    (b) relax
    (c) happy/delighted
    (d) birthday
    (e) husband

29. Celebrations
1   Any six: decide on guests, serve good variety of food, organise music, send invites in good time, write list of gifts, get outfit, go to hairdresser
2   (a) her group of friends/clique / better
    (b) 10 friends / expensive

30. Festivals
1   (a) NT, (b) R, (c) R, (d) F, (e) F, (f) NT, (g) F, (h) R

Local, national, international and global areas of interest

31. Home
1   (a) was sitting in front of the desk, rather than behind it
    (b) desk facing window to provide privacy / a screen from the room
    (c) with his back
    (d) behind him
    (e) that Charlie had invited him

32. Places to see
1   Lena: (a) six, (b) basement, (c) pictures/paintings, (d) streets
    Martin: (a) Sunday, (b) half past 8 in the morning/8.30 a.m., (c) beautiful views, (d) (any two:) picturesque look, sights, history

33. At the tourist office
1   B, D, G, H
2   C

34. Describing a town
1   (a) C, (b) B, (c) C, (d) A, (e) B, (f) C

35. Describing a region
1   1B, 2E, 3A, 4C, 5D

Sample answer / transcript

Teacher: Wo ist dein Wohnort?

Student: Ich wohne in einem Dorf im Nordwesten von England, in der Nähe von Liverpool. Die nächste Stadt in der Gegend heißt St Helens und sie hat ungefähr hunderttausend Einwohner.

Teacher: Was kann man in deiner Gegend machen?

Student: Hier im Dorf hat man viele Möglichkeiten: Man kann im Park Fußball spielen oder nach St Helens fahren und ins Stadion gehen, um ein Rugbyspiel zu sehen. Hier in der Gegend kann man auch ins Kino oder Theater gehen, und in der Stadt gibt es viele Restaurants und Nachtlokale.

Teacher: Was hast du am Wochenende in deiner Gegend gemacht?

Student: Am Samstag bin ich zuerst mit dem Bus in die Stadt gefahren, um neue Sportschuhe zu kaufen. Danach habe ich meine Freunde im Café getroffen und wir sind anschließend zusammen zum Skatepark gefahren. Das hat Spaß gemacht, obwohl das Wetter sehr kalt war.

Teacher: Was würdest du einem Touristen in deiner Gegend empfehlen?

Student: Als Tourist hier muss man unbedingt das Glasmuseum in St Helens besuchen, weil das sehr interessant ist. Ich würde auch einen Besuch an der Küste empfehlen, weil die Landschaft dort sehr eindrucksvoll ist. Es wäre auch gut, an einem Abend einmal ins Theater zu gehen.

Teacher: Was möchtest du an deiner Gegend ändern?

Student: Ich würde einen Freizeitpark in dieser Gegend bauen, weil der uns hier im Moment fehlt. Junge Leute würden das super finden, besonders, wenn man den Park einfach mit dem Bus von überall her erreichen könnte.

36. Volunteering
1   (a) Ich arbeite freiwillig.
    (b) Ich helfe in einem Altersheim.
    (c) Ich mache das jeden Samstag.
    (d) Die alten Leute erzählen interessante Geschichten.
    (e) Letztes Wochenende haben wir alle einen Geburtstag gefeiert.
2   Einmal im Monat arbeite ich freiwillig im Krankenhaus. Obwohl die Arbeit mir am Anfang gefallen hat, habe ich die Tage oft sehr anstrengend gefunden. Nächstes Jahr wird mein Bruder als Freiwilliger in einem Tierheim arbeiten. Er möchte sehr gern im Ausland mit Tieren arbeiten, die an einer Krankheiten leiden.

37. Charity work
1   (a) J, (b) L, (c) R
2   (a) C
    (b) im Tierheim

38. Social problems
1   (a) his best friend becoming homeless
    (b) want to help get people out of poverty
    (c) people to chat to / companionship / can discuss problems
    (d) nurse to talk to about worries / give advice
    (e) B
2   B, D, E

39. Healthy and unhealthy living
1   E, B, G, A
2   (a) Schokolade
    (b) Pizza ist billiger

SPEAKING TRACK 74

Listen to the recording

40. Healthy eating

1   A, C, F, I, K
2   (a) exhausted
     (b) had to buy the goods/fruit and veg first
     (c) Advantage: getting on with customers
        Disadvantage: adding up
     (d) good weather/sunshine

41. Feeling ill

1   (a) C, (b) A, (c) B, (d) C
2   (a) sitting on a tree trunk
     (b) the weather was especially lovely
     (c) one: unable to stand/get up / in terrible pain

42. Health issues

1   *Sample translation*
     I am sorry that my brother has been smoking since last year. I am afraid he will become addicted in time, but he claims that will never happen to him. My parents are naturally concerned about him, but despite this he still doesn't want to give up cigarettes. His friends smoke and he is under great pressure to do that as well, although this habit is very harmful.
2   *Sample translations*
     (a) Meine Eltern rauchen nicht.
     (b) Ich trinke nie Alkohol auf Festen/Partys.
     (c) Ich weiß, Drogen sind schädlich. / Ich weiß, dass Drogen schädlich sind.
     (d) Jugendliche/Junge Menschen können süchtig werden.
     (e) Letztes Jahr musste mein Onkel ins Krankenhaus (gehen).

43. Weather

1   (a) F, (b) F, (c) NT, (d) T, (e) F, (f) T, (g) NT, (h) T

44. Being green

1   *Sample translations*
     (a) Ich recycle immer Flaschen.
     (b) Ich fahre nie Rad.
     (c) Meine Eltern tragen immer Pullover im Haus.
     (d) Ich muss jetzt den Müll trennen / Jetzt muss ich den Müll trennen.
     (e) Sie hat geduscht anstatt zu baden, weil das umweltfreundlich war.
2   (a) to share their ideas on green living (you won't get a mark for saying they live an environmentally friendly life)
     (b) posts photos of environmental damage to woods/uploads photos of dreadful rubbish left in the woods
     (c) Daughter: (one:) writes own vegan recipes / gives make-up advice
     Son: (one:) gives energy saving tips for people to use at home / uploads videos to help

45. Protecting the environment

1   *Sample translation*
     The air pollution in my town is dreadful, especially when the weather is very hot. The airport is only five kilometres away from our flat and the motorway is also quite close. When I am older, I will definitely move to the countryside because the quality of life must be much better there. We should all protect the environment more by using public transport more often rather than travelling by car.
2   (a) B, (b) A

46. Natural resources

1   (a) A, (b) C, (c) C, (d) B, (e) A

47. Poverty

1   1B, 2E, 3D, 4A, 5C
3   *Sample answer / transcript*
     Teacher: Was gibt es auf dem Foto?
     Student: Das Bild zeigt Schüler in einem Land in Afrika, die sehr glücklich aussehen. Sie lächeln und

Listen to the recording

ich denke, sie sind vielleicht ein bisschen frech. Die Kinder tragen nicht Schulkleidung. Das Fenster ist offen, weil jemand jetzt das Foto macht. Diese Klasse ist in Afrika, denke ich, und das Wetter ist warm und trocken. Ich weiß nicht, was sie heute gelernt haben, aber die Tafel rechts hilft im Unterricht.
Teacher: Sammelst du gern Geld für Menschen in Not?
Student: Mir ist es wichtig, Geld für andere zu sammeln, weil viele Familien in Armut leben und wir im Vergleich zu ihnen sehr reich sind. An unserer Schule haben wir oft Spendenaktionen und ich finde das toll. Zum Beispiel organisieren wir ein Benefiz-Konzert oder wir backen und verkaufen Kuchen und Kekse in der Pause. Jede Klasse sammelt Geld und am Ende des Jahres schicken wir einer Organisation das Geld.
Teacher: Wie hast du neulich Geld gesammelt?
Student: Letztes Jahr habe ich Geld für Tiere gesammelt, weil mir die sehr am Herzen liegen. Unsere Klasse hat während des ganzen Jahres viele Aktionen organisiert, um Geld für den Tierschutz in der Gegend zu sammeln, aber das Beste war der Spendenlauf im Park. Ich habe extra dafür im Sportverein trainiert und am Tag des Spendenlaufs war ich superfit. Ich bin die zehn Kilometer extrem schnell gelaufen und danach konnte ich Geld von Verwandten und Freunden für den Tierschutzverein sammeln.
Teacher: Wie kann man am besten Geld sammeln?
Student: Tja, das ist eine gute Frage. Der Spendenlauf hat mir besonders gut gefallen, aber manche Schüler sind nicht so sportlich und ich denke, sie nehmen lieber an einem Konzert oder einem Event teil. Man kann auch Geld sammeln, wenn man zu Hause Hausarbeit macht oder babysittet. Statt das Geld selbst zu behalten, gibt man es einem Wohltätigkeitsverein.
Teacher: Sollte man Geld für Tiere oder den Kampf gegen die Armut spenden?
Student: Ich bin totaler Tierfan, also denke ich, dass der Tierschutz am wichtigsten ist. Am besten hilft man auch Menschen, die in Armut leben oder Hunger leiden, aber das interessiert mich nicht so sehr. Wenn ich Geld sammeln wollte, würde ich es lieber für Tiere sammeln, weil sie sich nicht selber helfen können.

48. Global problems

1   (a) J, (b) F, (c) M, (d) T, (e) M
2   Two of: children not having breakfast / families living in poverty / unemployment

49. Travel

1   *Sample translations*
     (a) Mein Vater findet Autos praktisch.
     (b) Ich fahre lieber mit dem Bus.
     (c) Der Verkehr in meiner Stadt ist wirklich laut.
     (d) Meine Schwester mag Autos nicht. / Meine Schwester mag keine Autos.
     (e) Letzte Woche haben wir im Auto Karten gespielt.
2   *Sample translation*
     Meine Mutter hat jeden Tag / täglich eine lange Fahrt zum Büro. Letzte Woche hat ihr Auto eine Panne in der Nähe der Tankstelle gehabt. Sie muss jetzt mit dem Rad fahren, während das Auto in der Werkstatt ist. Ich wünsche mir, dass weniger Leute mit dem Auto fahren würden, weil die öffentlichen Verkehrsmittel hier so gut sind.

50. Countries

1   *Sample translation*
     At the moment I am planning a train trip to Italy. I can either go to the travel agency or research everything on the internet. I will in any case buy a tourist guide from the bookshop as the texts and pictures are very useful. Before I went to Turkey last year, I had spent many hours preparing and that was worth it.
2   (a) father encourages family to travel / father finds travel important
     (b) (one of the following:) happy, confident (with language)
     (c) (both:) go for walks / enjoy nature

51. Transport

1. (a) Straßenbahn
   (b) Kaiserallee
   (c) ein Dieb
   (d) ein fremder Mann/Herr
   (e) er ist klein und die Stadt ist groß
   (f) 4 Millionen
2. B, E, F

52. Directions

1. A, D, E, H
2. (a) carry straight on
   (b) take the second road on the right
   (c) go round the corner
   (d) the right-hand side

53. Tourism

1. *Sample translation*
   My parents often go on holiday. They like writing postcards and (they) post photos online. In the summer I am going/will go on a bus trip to the coast. I never go to an airport, because I don't like flying. Last year I went by train to Switzerland.
2. A, D, F

54. Holiday preferences

Sample answer / transcript

Teacher: Guten Tag. Wohin wollen Sie in Urlaub fahren?
Student: Ich interessiere mich für einen Urlaub in Spanien.
Teacher: Wie lange wollen Sie bleiben?
Student: Ich möchte eine Woche dort verbringen.
Teacher: Was für eine Unterkunft möchten Sie und warum?
Student: Ich möchte am liebsten in einem Hotel bleiben, weil das am bequemsten ist.
Teacher: Was haben Sie letztes Jahr im Urlaub gemacht?
Student: Ich habe die Sehenswürdigkeiten besucht.
Teacher: Schön.
Student: Was kostet der Urlaub, bitte?
Teacher: 600 Euro.

55. Hotels

Sample answer / transcript

Teacher: Was reservieren Sie und für wie lange?
Student: Ein Doppelzimmer für zwei Nächte, bitte.
Teacher: Wann kommen Sie an?
Student: Am Dienstag um sechs Uhr abends.
Teacher: Wie fahren Sie zum Hotel?
Student: Ich fahre mit dem Zug.
Teacher: Was machen Sie abends gern?
Student: Ich sehe gern fern oder ich gehe gern ins Theater.
Teacher: Schön.
Student: Wie viel kostet das Zimmer, bitte?
Teacher: Es kostet 125 Euro pro Nacht.

56. Campsites

1. (a) May
   (b) one: towels / sleeping bags
   (c) the nature is wonderful
   (d) quiet
   (e) all guests
   (f) the farmhouse
2. (a) it's in the best area
   (b) they have to be quiet at night / not make noise
   (c) will be in a hotel with discos/pool at night

57. Accommodation

1. (a) W, (b) G, (c) H, (d) B, (e) H
2. (a) C
   (b) parents rent a flat on the coast

58. Holiday destinations

1. A, D, E
2. (a) B, D
   (b) A, E

59. Holiday experiences

1. *Sample translation*
   My family goes on a skiing holiday every year. We love the mountains and the fresh snow. I am learning to snowboard/ learning snowboarding this year. On a sunny day the view is particularly lovely. Last time my sister unfortunately went to hospital.
2. Any two (action + reason):
   Was sollten Gäste nicht tun? ohne T-Shirt in den Dom gehen / Selfies in der Galerie machen
   Warum? um den Urlaubsort zu respektieren / ein besseres Verhältnis zu den Einheimischen zu haben
   Was sollten Gäste nicht tun: Gläser ins Schwimmbad nehmen / kleine Kinder alleine im Schlafzimmer lassen
   Warum: aus Sicherheitsgründen / um einen besseren Urlaub zu haben

60. Holiday activities

1. Student's own answer
2. 1c, 2d, 3a, 4b

61. Holiday plans

1. B, D, F, G
2. (a) two of the following: lots to see / excellent shopping / can practise English
   (b) one of the following: her cousin stayed with her / it's her turn (you won't get a mark for saying her aunt lives in America)
   (c) one of the following: change her plans / do something different / not study there

62. Holiday problems

1. (a) L, (b) S, (c) A, (d) D, (e) L
2. (a) F, (b) C, (c) E, (d) A

Current and future study and employment

63. School subjects

1. *Sample translations*
   (a) Ich finde Mathe schwierig/schwer/nicht einfach.
   (b) Ich mag Naturwissenschaften nicht/Ich mache Naturwissenschaften nicht gern.
   (c) Wir haben jeden Mittwoch Erdkunde/Geografie.
   (d) Unser Bruder findet Kunst sehr langweilig.
   (e) Ich habe gestern eine gute Note in Chemie bekommen. / Gestern habe ich eine gute Note in Chemie bekommen.
2. *Sample translation*
   Dieses Jahr lerne ich Italienisch und Französisch. Als wir in der Grundschule waren, haben wir keine Fremdsprachen gelernt / haben wir Sprachen nicht gelernt. Meine Klasse wird nächstes Semester auch Spanisch haben und wir werden nach Madrid reisen/fahren. Ich möchte sehr gern Latein machen / lernen, weil das für die Universität nützlich wäre.

64. Opinions about school

1. (a) F, (b) NT, (c) R, (d) R, (e) F, (f) R, (g) NT, (h) F
2. (a) one of the following: bullying / students don't feel safe
   (b) one of the following: disruptive students / students chatting / texting each other
   (c) become a dentist

65. Types of schools

1. B, D, F, G
2. (a) P, (b) P+N, (c) N, (d) P

66. Primary school
1 (a) L+S, (b) S
2 (a) A, (b) C, (c) B, (d) B

67. Class trips
1 *Sample translation*
In my school every class goes on a class trip once a year. Most trips take place in Germany but some students also go abroad. I would like to go to America most of all, but I know that that will never happen because of the expense. Although I had really looked forward to the week at the coast last year, I was then very disappointed on the day, because I was ill.
2 (a) D, C
   (b) A, D

68. School exchange
1 (a) P, (b) A, (c) K
2 (a) 2008
   (b) overcame language problems
   (c) one: Eastern European food / their own food / food specialities from home (you need to have the adjective Eastern European or something to indicate it is their own type of food to score a point here)
   (d) one: got to know Germany / informed Germans about their home country
   (e) a future in a peaceful world / peace

69. School events
Sample answer / transcript
Teacher: Welches Event gibt es an deiner Schule und wann findet es statt?
Student: Im Sommer findet immer ein großes Sportfest statt.
Teacher: Wie war das Event letztes Jahr?
Student: Es hat viel Spaß gemacht und ich habe eine Medaille gewonnen.
Teacher: Wie findest du Schulevents?
Student: Ich finde Schulevents toll, weil sie interessant und spannend sind.
Teacher: Was hast du letztes Jahr beim Schulevent gemacht?
Student: Ich habe Sport gemacht.
Teacher: Gut.
Student: Nimmst du gern an Events teil?
Teacher: Ja, sehr gern.

SPEAKING TRACK 78

Listen to the recording

70. School day
1 (a) 10 Minuten
   (b) halb zehn/09.30
   (c) er hat sein Lieblingsfach / Erdkunde
   (d) zu Hause/bei ihm
   (e) one of the following: geht nach Hause / spielt am Computer
2 (a) B, (b) A, (c) C

71. School facilities
1 *Sample translation*
Today we have chemistry in the laboratory. I prefer to do sport in the gym/sports hall. Our school is great because the food in the canteen tastes good/is tasty. On Tuesday I drank a can of cola in the art room. Early tomorrow morning I have to/must go to the headmaster/headteacher because of it.
2 (a) fünf
   (b) die Schüler
   (c) der dritte Lehrer
   (d) die Kinder/Schüler/Schülerinnen

72. School rules
1 Student's own answer
2 1 b + c, 2 d + a

73. Pressures at school
1 A, C, E, H

74. Future study
1 (a) one of the following: she is waiting for exam results / needs good results to get into the best (grammar) school
   (b) one of the following: they think she will have best chance of getting high grade in the Abitur/A-levels / it's the best in the area
   (c) one of the following: work experience at vet's / she would rather work with animals than people
   (d) in another town
   (e) C
2 Was könnte man tun? Two of the following: bei den Hausaufgaben helfen / Computerzeit reduzieren / Kinder mit zur Arbeit nehmen
   Warum? Two of the following: besser lernen / auf die Schularbeit konzentrieren / die Arbeitswelt verstehen

75. Training
1 (a) B, (b) C
2 (a) dad a chemist/pharmacist
   (b) very interested in animals
   (c) help people
   (d) looking for big salary

76. CV
1 1 D, 2 A, 3 E, 4 C, 5 B
2 *Sample answer / transcript*
Teacher: Was sind deine Charaktereigenschaften?
Student: Ich bin selbstbewusst und freundlich und ich finde, das sind wichtige Charaktereigenschaften, wenn man mit anderen Leuten arbeitet. Ich komme gut mit Leuten aus, weil ich tolerant und nicht egoistisch bin.
Teacher: Was für Arbeitserfahrung hast du schon gesammelt?
Student: Seit zwei Jahren trage ich einmal pro Woche eine Lokalzeitung in der Gegend aus. Das finde ich ziemlich anstrengend, weil die meisten Leute im Hochhaus wohnen und ich die Treppen immer hinauf- und hinuntergehen muss, um die Zeitungen abzuliefern.
Teacher: Was wirst du nach den Prüfungen machen?
Student: Diesen Sommer werde ich nach den Prüfungen Kurzurlaub machen, bevor ich im September in die Oberstufe gehe, um mit der Schule weiterzumachen. Ich werde Naturwissenschaften und Deutsch wählen, weil dies meine Lieblingsfächer sind.
Teacher: Wo würdest du gern in Zukunft arbeiten?
Student: Ich habe keine festen Pläne für die Arbeitswelt, aber ich meine, dass ich vielleicht Lehrer werden will, weil das ein guter Beruf ist. Natürlich werde ich zuerst auf die Uni gehen, um dafür qualifiziert zu sein.
Teacher: Was für einen Lebensstil möchtest du in zehn Jahren haben?
Student: In zehn Jahren möchte ich einen gut bezahlten Job haben, bei dem ich in den Ferien viel reisen kann. Ich möchte am allerliebsten nach Amerika reisen, weil ich noch nie dort war und mir das Land sehr aufregend vorkommt.

SPEAKING TRACK 79

Listen to the recording

77. Jobs
1 (a) there are so many options / an increasing number of choices
   (b) (any one:) with animals / people
   (c) (any one:) know it from books/everyday life / to stop all the unwanted questions
2 (a) Job: police officer. Opinion: tiring
   (b) Job: computer specialist. Opinion: good (no weekend work)
   (c) Job: butcher. Opinion: interesting (likes customers)

78. Professions

1 *Sample translation*
My mother is a vet. She works in the centre of town. Her work pleases her/She likes her work, because she always likes helping other people. Last week our dog had an accident. Tomorrow we will go to the park again for the first time.

2 (a) C, (b) B, (c) A

79. Job ambitions

1 (a) one of the following: prefer to do apprenticeship / earn a bit of money / prepare for the future (you won't get a mark for saying they want to be mechanics / plumbers)
  (b) one of the following: to get a good job / earn high salary / get a fast car/own flat
  (c) one of the following: there's a good selection / there are plenty
  (d) one of the following: doesn't matter what the weather is like / has air conditioning
  (e) B

80. Opinions about jobs

1 (a) T, (b) F, (c) NT, (d) T, (e) T, (f) F, (g) NT, (h) T
2 (a) a department store
  (b) (one:) impatient / rude
  (c) thirty days' annual leave / 30 days' holiday a year
  (d) promotion prospects are good

81. Job adverts

1 (a) (one:) nice colleagues / good work conditions
  (b) near to/by the cathedral
  (c) serving customers/clients to the best of their ability
2 A, C, F

82. Applying for a job

1 Student's own answer
2 1 (c), 2 (a), 3 (d), 4 (b)

83. Job interview

Sample answer / transcript

Listen to the recording

Teacher: Was für einen Job suchen Sie?
Student: Ich suche einen Job als Babysitterin.
Teacher: Wann wollen Sie arbeiten?
Student: Ich will im Sommer arbeiten.
Teacher: Wo arbeiten Sie im Moment?
Student: Im Restaurant.
Teacher: Warum sind Sie für diesen Job geeignet?
Student: Ich arbeite gern mit Kindern und ich kann gut kochen.
Teacher: Schön.
Student: Wie viel verdiene ich als Babysitterin?
Teacher: 12 Euro pro Stunde.

84. Part-time jobs

1 A, C, D, F, I, L
2 (a) 15
  (b) (two:) deliver newspapers / babysit / tutor
  (c) (one:) 8 hours per day / 40 hours per week

Grammar

85. Gender and plurals

1 (a) der Abfalleimer
  (b) das Kino
  (c) die Krankenschwester
  (d) der Rucksack
  (e) das Handy
  (f) das Restaurant
  (g) die Autobahn
  (h) der Sportlehrer
  (i) die Umwelt

2 (a) Das Haus ist modern.
  (b) Der Schüler heißt Max.
  (c) Die Schülerin heißt Demet.
  (d) Der Computer ist kaputt.
  (e) Der Zug fährt langsam.
  (f) Die Bank ist geschlossen.
  (g) Die Zeitung kostet 1 Euro.
  (h) Das Buch ist langweilig.

3 (a) Wir haben die Pizza gegessen.
  (b) Wir können das Krankenhaus sehen.
  (c) Ich mache die Hausaufgabe.
  (d) Vati kauft den Pullover.
  (e) Liest du das Buch?
  (f) Ich wasche den Wagen.

4 Haus S, Buch S, Männer P, Autos P, Häuser P, Supermarkt S, Tisch S, Mann S, Supermärkte P, Tische P, Handys P, Zimmer E, Bilder P, Computer E

86. Cases and prepositions

1 (a) um die Ecke
  (b) durch die Stadt
  (c) ohne ein Auto
  (d) für die Schule
  (e) für einen Freund
  (f) gegen die Wand
  (g) durch einen Wald
  (h) die Straße entlang

2 (a) mit dem Bus
  (b) seit dem Sommer
  (c) zu der Bank / zur Bank
  (d) nach der Party
  (e) bei einem Freund
  (f) von einem Onkel
  (g) gegenüber der Tankstelle
  (h) außer der Lehrerin
  (i) aus dem Raum

3 (a) wegen des Wetters
  (b) während der Stunde
  (c) trotz des Regens

87. Prepositions with accusative or dative

1 (a) Wir fahren in die Stadt.
  (b) Meine Schwester ist in der Schule.
  (c) Das Essen steht auf dem Tisch.
  (d) Ich steige auf die Mauer.
  (e) Wir hängen das Bild an die Wand.
  (f) Jetzt ist das Bild an der Wand.
  (g) Die Katze läuft hinter einen Schrank.
  (h) Wo ist die Katze jetzt? Hinter dem Schrank.
  (i) Die Bäckerei steht zwischen einem Supermarkt und einer Post.
  (j) Das Flugzeug fliegt über die / der Stadt.
  (k) Ich stelle die Flaschen in den Schrank.
  (l) Der Bus steht an der Haltestelle.

2 (a) Die Kinder streiten sich über das Fernsehprogramm.
    The children are arguing about the TV programme.
  (b) Wir freuen uns auf das Fest.
    We are looking forward to the festival / celebration.
  (c) Ich ärgere mich oft über die Arbeit.
    I often get cross about work.
  (d) Martin hat sich an die Sonne gewöhnt.
    Martin has got used to the sun.
  (e) Wie lange warten Sie auf die Straßenbahn?
    How long have you been waiting for the tram?

3 1 C
  2 E
  3 D
  4 B
  5 A

88. Dieser / jeder, kein / mein

1 (a) *this man* – dieser Mann
   (b) *with this man* – mit diesem Mann
   (c) *this woman* – diese Frau
   (d) *for this woman* – für diese Frau
   (e) *every animal* – jedes Tier
   (f) *on that animal* – auf jenem Tier
2 (a) Unsere Schwester heißt Monika.
   (b) Ich habe keinen Bruder.
   (c) Meine Schule ist nicht sehr groß.
   (d) Hast du deinen Laptop vergessen?
   (e) Wie ist Ihr Name, bitte? *(No ending necessary)*
   (f) Meine Lehrerin hat ihre Schulbücher nicht mit.
   (g) Wo steht Ihr Auto? *(No ending necessary)*
   (h) Wir arbeiten in unserem Büro.
   (i) Wo ist eure Wohnung? *(Note spelling change)*
   (j) Meine Lieblingsfächer sind Mathe und Informatik.
   (k) Wie heißt deine Freundin?
   (l) Leider haben wir keine Zeit.
   (m) Ihre E-Mail war nicht sehr höflich.
   (n) Olaf geht mit seinem Freund spazieren.
   (o) Adele singt ihre besten Hits.
   (p) Wo habt ihr euer Auto stehen lassen? *(No ending necessary)*
   (q) Ich habe keine Ahnung.
   (r) Ich habe keine Lust.
   (s) Das war mein Fehler.
   (t) Meiner Meinung nach …

89. Adjective endings

1 (a) Die intelligente Schülerin bekommt gute Noten.
   (b) Wir fahren mit dem nächsten Bus in die Stadt.
   (c) Hast du den gelben Vogel gesehen?
   (d) Der altmodische Lehrer ist streng.
   (e) Ich kaufe dieses schwarze Kleid.
   (f) Die neugebauten Reihenhäuser sind schön.
   (g) Heute gehen wir in den modernen Freizeitpark.
   (h) Wir müssen dieses schmutzige Fahrrad sauber machen.
   (i) Morgen gehen wir ins neue Einkaufszentrum.
   (j) Der verspätete Zug kommt um 1 Uhr an.
2 (a) München ist eine umweltfreundliche Stadt.
   (b) Ich suche ein preiswertes T-Shirt.
   (c) Marta hat ihre modische Handtasche verloren.
   (d) Wir haben unsere schwierigen Hausaufgaben nicht gemacht.
   (e) Ich habe ein bequemes Bett gekauft.
   (f) Das ist ein großes Problem.
   (g) Das war vielleicht eine langweilige Stunde!
   (h) Diese idiotischen Leute haben das Spiel verdorben.
   (i) Mein Vater hat einen schweren Unfall gehabt.
   (j) Klaus liebt seine neue Freundin.
   (k) Wir haben kein frisches Obst.
   (l) Maria hat einen grünen Mantel gekauft.

90. Comparisons

1 (a) Mathe ist langweilig, Physik ist langweiliger, aber das langweiligste Fach ist Kunst.
   (b) Oliver läuft schnell, Ali läuft schneller, aber Tim läuft am schnellsten.
   (c) Berlin ist schön, Paris ist schöner, aber Wien ist die schönste Stadt.
   (d) Rihanna ist cool, Katy Perry ist cooler, aber Taylor Swift ist die coolste Sängerin.
   (e) Metallica ist lauter als Motörhead.
   (f) Bremen ist kleiner als Hamburg.
   (g) Deine Noten sind schlecht, aber meine sind noch schlechter.
   (h) Ich finde Englisch einfacher als Französisch, aber Deutsch finde ich am einfachsten.
   (i) Skifahren ist schwieriger als Radfahren.
   (j) Mein Auto ist billiger als dein Auto, aber das Auto meines Vaters ist am billigsten.

2 (a) Ich bin jünger als du.
       I am younger than you.
   (b) Die Alpen sind höher als der Snowdon.
       The Alps are higher than Snowdon.
   (c) München ist größer als Bonn.
       Munich is bigger than Bonn.
   (d) Meine Haare sind lang, Timos Haare sind länger, aber deine Haare sind am längsten.
       My hair is long, Timo's hair is longer, but your hair is the longest.
   (e) Fußball ist gut, Handball ist besser, aber Tennis ist das beste Spiel.
       Football is good, handball is better, but tennis is the best game.
3 (a) Ich spiele gern Basketball.
   (b) Ich esse lieber Gemüse als Fleisch.
   (c) Am liebsten gehe ich schwimmen.

91. Personal pronouns

1 (a) Ich liebe dich.
   (b) Liebst du mich?
   (c) Kommst du mit mir?
   (d) Mein Bruder ist nett. Ich mag ihn gern.
   (e) Ich habe keine Kreditkarte. Ich habe sie verloren.
   (f) Ein Geschenk für uns? Danke!
   (g) Wir haben euch gestern gesehen.
   (h) Haben Sie gut geschlafen?
   (i) Die Party ist bei mir.
   (j) Rolf hatte Hunger. Ich bin mit ihm essen gegangen.
   (k) Vergiss mich nicht!
   (l) Wie heißt du?
   (m) Wie heißen Sie?
   (n) Meine Schwester ist krank. Gestern sind wir zu ihr gegangen.
2 (a) Schwimmen fällt mir schwer.
   (b) Mmmm, Eis! Schmeckt es dir?
   (c) Aua! Das tut mir weh!
   (d) Leider geht es uns nicht gut.
   (e) Wer gewinnt im Fußball? Das ist mir egal.
   (f) Es tut uns leid.

92. Word order

1 (a) Um 6 Uhr beginnt die Fernsehsendung.
   (b) Jeden Tag fahre ich mit dem Bus zur Arbeit.
   (c) Leider sind meine Eltern krank.
   (d) Hier darf man nicht rauchen.
2 (a) Gestern haben wir Eis gegessen.
   (b) Manchmal ist Timo ins Kino gegangen.
   (c) Letztes Jahr ist Ali nach Frankreich gefahren.
   (d) Heute Morgen hast du Pommes gekauft.
3 (a) Ich fahre jeden Tag mit dem Rad zur Schule.
   (b) Gehst du am Wochenende mit mir zum Schwimmbad?
   (c) Wir sehen oft im Wohnzimmer fern.
   (d) Mehmet spielt abends Tischtennis im Jugendclub.
   (e) Mein Vater arbeitet seit 20 Jahren fleißig im Büro.
   (f) Willst du heute Abend mit mir im Restaurant Pizza essen?

93. Conjunctions

1 (a) Claudia will Sportlehrerin werden, weil sie sportlich ist.
   (b) Ich kann dich nicht anrufen, weil mein Handy nicht funktioniert.
   (c) Wir fahren nach Spanien, weil das Wetter dort so schön ist.
   (d) Du darfst nicht im Garten spielen, weil es noch regnet.
   (e) Peter hat seine Hausaufgaben nicht gemacht, weil er faul ist.
   (f) Ich mag Computerspiele, weil sie so aufregend sind.
2 (a) Du kannst abwaschen, während ich koche.
   (b) Wir kaufen oft ein, wenn wir in der Stadt sind.
   (c) Ich kann nicht zur Party kommen, da ich arbeiten werde.
   (d) Lasst uns früh aufstehen, damit wir wandern können.
   (e) Meine Eltern waren böse, obwohl ich nicht spät nach Hause gekommen bin.

(f) Ich habe es nicht gewusst, dass du krank bist.

(g) Papa hat geraucht, als er jung war.

(h) Ich weiß nicht, wie man einen Computer repariert.

(i) Wir können schwimmen gehen, wenn das Wetter gut ist.

(j) Wir müssen warten, bis es nicht mehr regnet.

94. More on word order

1 (a) Wir fahren in die Stadt, um Lebensmittel zu kaufen.

(b) Viele Leute spielen Tennis, um fit zu werden.

(c) Boris spart Geld, um ein Motorrad zu kaufen.

(d) Meine Schwester geht zur Abendschule, um Französisch zu lernen.

(e) Ich bin gestern zum Imbiss gegangen, um Pommes zu essen.

2 (a) Das Orchester beginnt zu spielen.

(b) Wir hoffen, Spanisch zu lernen.

(c) Oliver versucht, Gitarre zu spielen.

3 (a) das Mädchen, das Tennis spielt

(b) der Junge, der gut singt

(c) der Mann, der Deutsch spricht

(d) das Haus, das alt ist

(e) das Fach, das schwer ist

(f) das Auto, das kaputt ist

(g) die Tasse, die voll ist

95. The present tense

1 (a) wir gehen

(b) er findet

(c) sie singt

(d) ich spiele

(e) ihr macht

(f) du sagst

(g) es kommt

(h) sie schwimmen

(i) ich höre

(j) wir trinken

2 (a) Was liest du?
    What are you reading?

(b) Schläfst du?
    Are you asleep?

(c) Annabelle isst nicht gern Fleisch.
    Annabelle doesn't like eating meat.

(d) Kerstin spricht gut Englisch.
    Kerstin speaks English well.

(e) Nimmst du Zucker?
    Do you take sugar?

(f) Ben fährt bald nach Berlin.
    Ben is going to Berlin soon.

(g) Hilfst du mir, bitte?
    Will you help me please?

(h) Mein Onkel gibt mir 20 Euro.
    My uncle is giving me 20 euros.

3 er spricht, du siehst, sie fährt, er liest

96. Separable and reflexive verbs

1 (a) Wir kommen bald an.

(b) Er fährt um 7 Uhr ab.

(c) Wir laden oft Filme herunter.

(d) Wie oft siehst du fern?

(e) Wo steigt man aus?

(f) Ich mache die Tür zu.

2 (a) Wir sind bald angekommen.

(b) Er ist um 7 Uhr abgefahren.

(c) Wir haben oft Filme heruntergeladen.

(d) Wie oft hast du ferngesehen?

(e) Wo ist man ausgestiegen?

(f) Ich habe die Tür zugemacht.

3 (a) Ich interessiere mich für Geschichte.
    I am interested in history.

(b) Sara freut sich auf die Ferien.
    Sara is looking forward to the holidays.

(c) Erinnerst du dich an mich?
    Do you remember me?

(d) Wir langweilen uns in der Schule.
    We get bored at school.

(e) Ich habe mich noch nicht entschieden.
    I haven't decided yet.

(f) Tina hat sich heute nicht geschminkt.
    Tina hasn't put on make-up today.

(g) Habt ihr euch gut amüsiert?
    Have you enjoyed yourselves?

(h) Unser Haus befindet sich in der Nähe vom Bahnhof.
    Our house is situated near the train station.

97. Commands

1 (a) Parken Sie hier nicht!

(b) Sprechen Sie nicht so laut!

(c) Steigen Sie hier aus!

(d) Fahren Sie nicht so schnell!

(e) Kommen Sie herein!

(f) Gehen Sie geradeaus!

(g) Kommen Sie bald wieder!

(h) Geben Sie mir 10 Euro!

2 (a) Steh auf!

(b) Schreib bald!

(c) Komm her!

(d) Nimm zwei!

(e) Bring mir den Ball!

(f) Hör auf!

(g) Benimm dich!

(h) Setz dich!

98. Present tense modals

1 (a) Ich kann nicht schnell laufen.

(b) Wir müssen bald Kaffee kaufen.

(c) Kinder sollen keinen Alkohol trinken.

(d) Claudia mag nicht schwimmen.

(e) Schüler dürfen hier nicht sitzen.

(f) Wir wollen Pommes essen.

(g) Hier darf man parken.

(h) Meine Eltern wollen eine neue Wohnung mieten.

(i) Du kannst gut Fußball spielen.

(j) Sie sollten höflich sein.

2 (a) Im Kino darf man nicht rauchen.

(b) Wir möchten zur Bowlingbahn gehen.

(c) Meine Freunde wollen zu Hause bleiben.

(d) Ihr müsst weniger essen.

(e) Man soll nicht viel Zucker essen.

(f) Ergül kann gut Gitarre spielen.

(g) Kannst du mir bei meinen Hausaufgaben helfen?

(h) Man darf hier nie spielen.

(i) Wir müssen mit der Straßenbahn fahren.

(j) Ich will meinen Salat nicht essen.

99. Imperfect modals

1 (a) ich wollte   (e) man sollte
    (b) wir mussten   (f) er mochte
    (c) sie konnten   (g) wir wollten
    (d) sie durfte   (h) Jutta konnte

2 (a) Du solltest gesund essen.

(b) Wir mussten nach Hause gehen.

(c) Ella mochte nicht Musik hören.

(d) Wir wollten im Internet surfen.

(e) Ich konnte gut Tischtennis spielen.

(f) Ihr durftet spät ins Bett gehen.

3 (a) Möchten Sie Tennis spielen?

(b) Wir könnten einkaufen gehen.

(c) Ich möchte ein Eis essen.

(d) Könntest du mir helfen?

100. The perfect tense 1

1 (a) Wir haben Minigolf gespielt.

(b) Habt ihr neue Schuhe gekauft?

(c) Hast du deine Oma besucht?

(d) Was hat er gesagt?

(e) Ich habe Spanisch gelernt.
(f) Hast du diese Zeitung gelesen?
(g) Dennis hat mir ein Geschenk gegeben.
(h) Wir haben einen tollen Film gesehen.
2 (a) Wohin bist du gefahren?
   (b) Wir sind nach Mallorca gefahren.
   (c) Ich bin zu Hause geblieben.
   (d) Usain Bolt ist schnell gelaufen.
   (e) Meine Mutter ist nach Amerika geflogen.
   (f) Der Zug ist abgefahren.
3 (a) Abdul hat 12 Stunden geschlafen.
   (b) Wir haben unsere Hausaufgaben gemacht.
   (c) Wohin bist du gefahren?
   (d) Ich bin spät nach Hause gekommen.
   (e) Habt ihr Britta gesehen?

101. The perfect tense 2
1 (a) geschwommen   (i) gesprochen
   (b) gewesen   (j) getroffen
   (c) geschlossen   (k) geworden
   (d) gegessen   (l) getrunken
   (e) gestanden   (m) genommen
   (f) gesessen   (n) gesungen
   (g) geschrieben   (o) gehabt
   (h) gestorben
2 (a) Wir haben eine E-Mail geschrieben.
   (b) Wir haben uns um 6 Uhr getroffen.
   (c) Niemand ist gestorben.
   (d) Hast du mein Handy genommen?
   (e) Ich habe eine Bratwurst gegessen.
   (f) Er hat ein Glas Cola getrunken.
   (g) Wir sind im Meer geschwommen.
   (h) Marita hat Italienisch gesprochen.
3 (a) vergessen   (e) besucht
   (b) angekommen   (f) heruntergeladen
   (c) empfohlen   (g) abgefahren
   (d) verloren   (h) ausgestiegen

102. The imperfect tense
1 (a) Ich spielte am Computer.
   (b) Was sagtest du?
   (c) Nina kaufte Chips.
   (d) Die Schüler lernten Englisch.
   (e) Es schneite im Winter.
   (f) Peter lachte laut.
2 (a) Es war gestern kalt.
   (b) Wir hatten auf der Party viel Spaß.
   (c) Paul war im Krankenhaus.
   (d) Meine Eltern hatten drei Kinder.
   (e) Ich war gestern im Imbiss.
   (f) Hattest du Angst?
3 (a) Es gab viel zu essen. I
   (b) Wir sitzen im Kino. P
   (c) Es tut mir leid! P
   (d) Ich fahre nach Berlin. P
   (e) Er kommt früh an. P
   (f) Er saß im Wohnzimmer. I
   (g) Sie kamen um 6 Uhr an. I
   (h) Wie findest du das? P
   (i) Aua! Das tat weh! I
   (j) Ich fand es gut. I
   (k) Es gibt nicht viel zu tun. P
   (l) Klaus fuhr zu schnell. I

103. The future tense
1 (a) Susi geht nächstes Jahr auf die Uni.
   (b) Wir fahren im Sommer nach Ibiza.
   (c) Er kommt übermorgen zu uns.
   (d) Ich bleibe heute Abend zu Hause.
   (e) Bringst du am Wochenende deine Schwester mit?

2 (a) Ich werde um 6 Uhr abfahren.
   (b) Wirst du am Wochenende Musik hören?
   (c) Werdet ihr Pizza essen?
   (d) Wir werden die Prüfung bestehen.
   (e) Nächstes Jahr werden wir nach Afrika reisen.
   (f) Daniel wird einen Film herunterladen.
   (g) Ich werde ein Problem mit meinem Laptop haben.
   (h) Bayern München wird das Spiel gewinnen.
   (i) Meine Freunde werden um 9 Uhr ankommen.
   (j) Meine Schwester wird im August heiraten.
3 Your own answers

104. The conditional
1 (a) Wenn wir Zeit hätten, würden wir einkaufen gehen.
   (b) Wenn meine Eltern Geld hätten, würden sie ein Auto kaufen.
   (c) Wenn ich Kinder hätte, würde ich sie lieben.
   (d) Wenn Tanja nicht krank wäre, würde sie Skateboard fahren.
   (e) Wenn du fleißiger wärst, würdest du deine Prüfung bestehen.
   (f) Wenn das Wetter besser wäre, würden wir Sport treiben.
2 (a) Wenn ich Krankenschwester wäre, würde ich mich freuen.
   (b) Wenn er Klempner wäre, würde er viel verdienen.
   (c) Wenn wir in einer Fabrik arbeiten würden, wären wir müde.
   (d) Wenn wir Glasflaschen hätten, würden wir sie recyceln.
   (e) Wenn ich Hunger hätte, würde ich eine Bratwurst essen.
   (f) Wenn Manya und Timo Talent hätten, würden sie in einer Band spielen.
3 Your own answers
4 Your own answers

105. The pluperfect tense
1 (a) Wir hatten Kaffee und Kuchen bestellt.
   (b) Hattest du Spaß gehabt?
   (c) Ich hatte eine neue Stelle bekommen.
   (d) Wir hatten unsere Freunde eingeladen.
   (e) Als ich nach Hause gekommen war, habe ich gegessen.
   (f) Kagan war zur Bäckerei gegangen.
   (g) Sie waren zu Hause geblieben.
   (h) Ich war mit dem Auto nach Frankfurt gefahren.
2 (a) Es war nicht passiert.
   (b) Ich hatte dir eine E-Mail geschickt.
   (c) Hattest du dich nicht geschminkt?
   (d) Ich war sehr früh eingeschlafen.
   (e) Opa war noch nie nach London gefahren.
   (f) Warst du zur Haltestelle gegangen?
   (g) Wir hatten unseren Müll zur Mülldeponie gebracht.
   (h) Er hatte zwei Computerspiele heruntergeladen.
   (i) Die Fabrik war sehr laut gewesen.
   (j) Fatima hatte Abitur gemacht.

106. Questions
1 (a) Spielt Kevin oft am Computer?
   (b) Hast du dein Handy verloren?
   (c) Wollen wir Volleyball spielen?
   (d) Studiert Hakan Informatik?
   (e) Geht ihr morgen zum Sportzentrum?
2 (a) Bist du zum Supermarkt gefahren?
   (b) Wird Ayse Chemie studieren?
   (c) Ist dein Auto kaputt?
   (d) Isst du gern Bratwurst mit Pommes?
   (e) Wird es morgen regnen?
3 *who?* – wer? *what?* – was? *how?* – wie?
   when? – wann? *why?* – warum? *where?* – wo?
   how many? – wie viele? *what kind of?* – was für?
   whose? – wessen? *who with?* – mit wem?
4 Your own answers

107. Time markers

1   (a) gestern – *past*
    (b) früher – *past*
    (c) bald – *future*
    (d) letzte Woche – *past*
    (e) heute – *present*
    (f) normalerweise – *present*
    (g) vor zwei Wochen – *past*
    (h) morgen – *future*
    (i) nächste Woche – *future*
    (j) jetzt – *present*

2   1 C, 2 E, 3 A, 4 F, 5 B, 6 D

3   (a) Nächste Woche werde ich mein Betriebspraktikum machen.
    (b) Heute Abend sieht Ulli fern.
    (c) In Zukunft wird man Strom sparen.
    (d) Bald wirst du einen Unfall haben.
    (e) Manchmal treffen wir uns mit unseren Freunden.
    (f) Neulich war ich bei meinem Onkel.
    (g) Vorgestern hat Metin sein Betriebspraktikum begonnen.
    (h) Jeden Tag gehe ich zur Bäckerei.

108. Numbers

1   (a) 421
    (b) 1644
    (c) 68
    (d) 301
    (e) 97
    (f) 105
    (g) 17
    (h) 653

2   (a) Es ist zwanzig nach neun. (20, 9)
    (b) Ausverkauf! Fünfzehn Prozent Rabatt! (15)
    (c) Es ist dreizehn Grad. (13)
    (d) Ich habe sechshundertfünfzig Euro gewonnen. (650)
    (e) Der Zug kommt um zwölf Minuten vor sieben an. (12, 7)
    (f) Es gibt dreißig Schüler in meiner Klasse. (30)

3   (a) 12.3.   (b) 13.7.   (c) 28.12.
    (d) 1.4.   (e) 3.1.   (f) 17.6.

4   (a) Mein Geburtstag ist am ersten November.
    (b) Saschas Geburtstag ist am siebten September.
    (c) Das Konzert findet am zwölften Mai statt.
    (d) Die Ferien beginnen am zweiten Juli.

Practice tests

109. Practice test: Listening 1

1   (a) C, (b) A, (c) C

2   Mia's work placement wish: work in a school
    Luka's opinion: (quite) boring

110. Practice test: Listening 2

1   (a) in primary school
    (b) prefers to sit in front of screen alone
    (c) trip to the theme park
    (d) boss/director of a global firm

2   (a) B
    (b) Familien lieben es

111. Practice test: Listening 3

1   (a) one of the following: so quiet in class he wasn't noticed/
    never wanted to answer a question
    (b) one of the following: she likes him now/happy to go to
    school with him / no longer avoids him
    (c) two of the following: cheeky, talkative/got detentions/
    rarely did homework/had to go to head
    (d) has a nicer new group of friends

2   B, C, F

112. Practice test: Speaking 1

Sample answer / transcript

1   **Teacher:** An welchem Tag wollen Sie fahren?
    Student: Ich will am Montag fahren, bitte.
    Teacher: Um wie viel Uhr wollen Sie abfahren?
    Student: Ich will um elf Uhr dreißig abfahren.
    Teacher: Was für eine Fahrkarte wollen Sie kaufen?
    Student: Ich will eine einfache Karte kaufen, bitte.
    Teacher: Warum fahren Sie dorthin?
    Student: Ich besuche Freunde.
    Teacher: Sehr gut.
    Student: Wie viel kostet die Fahrkarte, bitte?
    Teacher: 45 Euro.

Sample answer / transcript

2   **Teacher:** Was hast du gestern online gemacht?
    Student: Ich habe mit Freunden gechattet.
    Teacher: Wie findest du Computerspiele?
    Student: Ich finde sie fantastisch, weil sie unterhaltsam sind.
    Teacher: Was findest du schlecht an Online-Aktivitäten?
    Student: Man kann unter Internet-Mobbing leiden.
    Teacher: Wie oft benutzt du einen Computer?
    Student: Jeden Tag.
    Teacher: Interessant.
    Student: Was machen wir nach dem Abendessen am Computer?
    Teacher: Wir hören Musik.

113. Practice test: Speaking 2

Foundation

Sample answer / transcript

Teacher: Was gibt es auf dem Foto?
Student: Dieses Foto ist interessant, finde ich. Die vier Leute interessieren sich sehr für den Umweltschutz, denke ich. Sie sammeln hier Abfall, um diese Gegend zu verbessern. Das Wetter ist kalt und windig, aber sie tragen warme Kleidung. Vielleicht finden sie alte Dosen und Plastiktüten, die Leute hier weggeworfen haben.
Teacher: Wie kann man die Umwelt schützen?
Student: Ich versuche, umweltfreundlich zu sein und ich trenne gern den Müll zu Hause. Im Winter spare ich Energie, weil ich die Heizung nie hoch stelle. Ich ziehe lieber einen warmen Pullover an. Am liebsten fahre ich mit dem Rad in die Stadt, weil ich das Autofahren schrecklich finde.
Teacher: Wie umweltfreundlich warst du letzte Woche?
Student: Letzte Woche habe ich mich geduscht. So habe ich Wasser gespart. Ich habe meine alten T-Shirts zum Container gebracht, um sie zu recyceln. Ich bin überall mit dem Rad gefahren.
Teacher: Wie bist du im Urlaub umweltfreundlich?
Student: Ich fliege nie mit dem Flugzeug und ich fahre nur manchmal mit dem Auto in den Urlaub, denn das ist sehr umweltschädlich. Ich übernachte am liebsten in einem Naturpark oder auf einem Campingplatz am Meer. Hotels finde ich nicht gut für die Umwelt.
Teacher: Was macht deine Familie, um der Umwelt zu helfen?
Student: Als Familie protestieren wir alle gegen das Aussterben von Tieren. Wir lieben Tiere und glauben, wir müssen alle Tierarten schützen. Unserer Meinung nach sind Tiere wichtiger als Menschen. Meinen Sie das auch?

Higher

Sample answer / transcript

Teacher: Was gibt es auf dem Foto?
Student: Dieses Foto ist interessant und ich stelle mir vor, man hat es in der Nähe

einer Großstadt gemacht. Die vier Leute interessieren sich sehr für den Umweltschutz und machen sich Sorgen um unseren Planeten. Deshalb sammeln sie hier Abfall, um diese Gegend zu verbessern. Sie machen das, obwohl das Wetter kalt und windig ist. Vielleicht finden sie alte Dosen und Plastiktüten, die faule Besucher nicht mit nach Hause genommen haben.

Teacher: Wie wichtig ist dir Umweltschutz?

Student: Also, ich bin ziemlich umweltfreundlich, und so wie andere auch, trenne ich den Müll in der Schule und zu Hause, aber sonst mache ich nicht so viel, muss ich sagen. Ich finde es gut, dass man an der Kasse für Plastiktüten bezahlen muss, aber ich fahre immer noch lieber mit dem Auto als mit dem Rad.

Teacher: Wie möchtest du in Zukunft der Umwelt helfen?

Student: Da könnte ich noch Vieles machen, aber ich hoffe erstens, nächsten Monat an der Fahrradwoche an unserer Schule teilzunehmen. Zu Hause hoffe ich, danach einen Nistkasten für Vögel zu bauen, aber ich bin kein begabter Tischler, also werde ich das vielleicht nie machen!

Teacher: Ist es wichtiger Tiere oder Pflanzen zu schützen?

Student: Das ist eine gute Frage! Ohne Pflanzen können wir nicht überleben, meine ich, also sind Pflanzen wahrscheinlich wichtiger als Tiere. Aber ich liebe alle Tiere und finde sie auf der anderen Seite wichtiger als Pflanzen. Wie stehen Sie zu dieser Frage?

Teacher: Möchtest du für eine Umweltorganisation arbeiten? Warum oder warum nicht?

Student: Also für mich ist das ohne Zweifel eine ausgezeichnete Idee, aber in der Zukunft möchte ich Tierarzt werden. Meiner Ansicht nach ist ein hohes Gehalt sehr wichtig, und wenn ich für eine Umweltorganisation arbeiten würde, würde ich zu wenig Geld verdienen.

114. Practice test: Reading 1

1   (a) H, (b) L, (c) F
2   *Sample translation*
    My mother always saves energy. At home we all wear warm jumpers. That is annoying, because I prefer to wear T-shirts. Last Wednesday I didn't separate/sort the rubbish. Next week I will do that every day.

115. Practice test: Reading 2

1   (a) there is a wide variety of sport offered at school
    (b) one of the following: leading a healthy life / training regularly / doing sport
    (c) one of the following: they have sports clubs/school sports clubs / sports clubs didn't exist before
    (d) it will create an active country
2   (a) F, (b) NT, (c) T, (d) T, (e) T, (f) NT, (g) T, (h) NT

116. Practice test: Reading 3

1   A, D, F, G

117. Practice test: Reading 4

1   (a) wegen der Frau seines Vaters/weil sein Vater eine neue Frau hat
    (b) seit 4 Jahren
    (c) one of the following: dass er babysitten musste / dass er nicht mit Freunden ins Kino gehen durfte
    (d) mit seiner älteren Schwester
    (e) one of the following: sie wohnt nicht mehr zu Hause / er kann nicht mit ihr reden, wann er will
2   *Sample translation*
    My father is a doctor in the country(side), although he doesn't like this job. He often has to work nights and then he comes back home exhausted. He would much prefer to have another position/job where the hours are shorter. Before he became a doctor, he had a part-time job in a shop in the town centre, which he really enjoyed/liked.

118. Practice test: Writing 1

1   *Sample answer*
    Ich verbringe eine Woche auf dem Campingplatz. Ich schlafe gern im Zelt. Morgens wache ich sehr früh auf. Morgen machen wir eine Wanderung.
2   *Sample answer:*
    Unsere Schule befindet sich zwei Kilometer von der Stadtmitte entfernt. Sie ist eine gut ausgestattete Schule und wir haben eine große Aula. In der Pause kann man etwas in der Kantine kaufen oder auf dem Schulhof spielen. Nächste Woche gibt es ein Musikfest, wo alle Schüler an Konzerten teilnehmen.

119. Practice test: Writing 2

1   *Sample translation*
    (a) Ich esse gern Pommes (Frites).
    (b) Mein Bruder isst nie Fleisch.
    (c) Meine Lieblingsnachspeise ist Kuchen mit Schokoladensoße.
    (d) Mein Lehrer/Meine Lehrerin muss ins Krankenhaus gehen.
    (e) Am Wochenende habe ich eine Flasche Cola getrunken.
2   *Sample translation*
    Letztes Jahr zu Ostern haben meine Eltern viele Eier im Garten versteckt. Jedes Mal, als ich ein Ei gefunden habe, hat mein Bruder es mir sofort weggenommen. Nächstes Jahr werde ich keine Schokolade suchen, weil sie sehr ungesund ist. Ich würde das Geld lieber für Kleider ausgeben, die viel nützlicher sind.

120. Practice test: Writing 3

1   *Sample answer*
    Hallo Sadi,
    ich wohne seit drei Jahren in einer großen Wohnung im dritten Stock eines modernen Hochhauses. Letztes Wochenende habe ich viele Stunden in meinem Schlafzimmer an der Konsole verbracht, weil das Wetter so schlecht war. In den Sommerferien gehe ich oft in den Sportverein, um dort Fußball mit Freunden zu spielen. Ich finde das gesünder, als immer drinnen zu bleiben. Du musst mich bald besuchen, weil die Gegend hier echt schön ist. Wir können zusammen ins Freibad gehen oder eine Radtour machen. Das macht mir immer Spaß!
    Dein(e) X

121. Practice test: Writing 4

1   *Sample answer*
    Nächsten Monat nehme ich an einem Marathonlauf in der Stadt teil, um Geld für ein wertvolles Wasserprojekt in Westafrika zu sammeln. Das originelle Wasserprojekt befindet sich in einem kleinen Dorf, wo die Frauen und Kinder früher zehn Kilometer zum Wasserholen gehen mussten. Mit Hilfe des Wasserprojektes fließt in ihrem Dorf seit drei Jahren frisches Trinkwasser. Wir möchten jetzt ein ähnliches Wasserprojekt für ein anderes Dorf in der Gegend organisieren und dafür bitte ich Sie heute um Spenden. Letztes Jahr habe ich viel Geld in der Schule für dieses Projekt gesammelt, indem ich Kuchen gebacken habe und gesponserte Aktivitäten gemacht habe. Dieses Jahr ist es mein Ziel, am Marathonlauf teilzunehmen, und es würde mich sehr freuen, wenn Ihre Firma etwas für diesen guten Zweck spenden könnte. Am Tag des Laufes werde ich ein bunt gestreiftes T-Shirt tragen und ich könnte das Logo Ihrer Firma ganz groß darauf drucken, wenn Sie mir Geld spenden würden.

Published by Pearson Education Limited, 80 Strand, London, WC2R 0RL.

www.pearsonschoolsandfecolleges.co.uk

Text and illustrations © Pearson Education Ltd 2017
Typeset and illustrated by Kamae Design, Oxford
Produced by Out of House Publishing
Cover illustration by Miriam Sturdee

The right of Harriette Lanzer to be identified as author of this work has been asserted by her in accordance with the Copyright, Designs and Patents Act 1988.

First published 2017

20 19 18 17
10 9 8 7 6 5 4 3 2

British Library Cataloguing in Publication Data
A catalogue record for this book is available from the British Library

ISBN 978 1 292 13138 2

Printed by Neografia in Slovakia

Acknowledgements
The publisher would like to thank the following for their kind permission to reproduce copyright material:

Text
Page 30: Astrid Lindgren, Pelle zieht aus und andere Weihnachtsgeschichten, © 1985 Verlag Friedrich Oetinger, Hamburg. Used with permission of Oetinger.

Page 31: Die neuen Leiden des jungen W. by Ulrich Plenzdorf, Harrap's modern World Literature Series, first published 1973, Used by permission of Pushkin Press.

Page 46: Vanessa Farquharson, Nackt schlafen ist bio: Eine Öko-Zynikerin findet ihr Grünes Gewissen und die große Liebe, Bastei Lübbe 2011. Used with permission of Bastei Lübbe.

Page 73: Juma Kliebenstein, Der Tag, an dem ich cool wurde, © 2010 Verlag Friedrich Oetinger, Hamburg. Used with permission of Oetinger.

Photos
(Key: b-bottom; c-centre; l-left; r-right; t-top)

123RF.com: Anthony Baggett 78/(c) C, Dmitry Kalinovsky 78/(b) C, Dmitry Travnikov 8, dolgachov 67/(b) D, highwaystarz 10b, HONGQI ZHANG 78/(c) B, JarenWicklund 24cl, kaliantye 45bc, Konstantin Chagin 67/(b) B, lenanet 37br, mexitographer 45bl, mihtiander 78/(a) B, Nattee Chalermtiragool 33l, sam74100 66tr, Wavebreak Media Ltd 78/(c) A; **Alamy Stock Photo:** aberCPC 113, Bananastock 78/(b) B, David Wall 67/(a) C, JTB MEDIA CREATION, Inc. 33c, Juice Images 20, Kumar Sriskandan 67/(a) A, LOOK Die Bildagentur der Fotografen GmbH 56t, MBI 11, Pawel Kazmierczak 56b, RosaIreneBetancourt 4 26, Ulrich Doering 47; **Datacraft Co Ltd:** 67/(b) C; **Fotolia.com:** Halfpoint 15; **Getty Images:** David Leahy 17; **Pearson Education Ltd:** Studio 8 6, Jon Barlow 66cr, Jörg Carstensen 78/(a) C, Jules Selmes 67/(a) B, Tudor Photography 109/B; **Photolibrary.com:** Corbis / Randy Faris 67/(b) A; **Press Association Images:** David Klein / Sportimage 18l; **Shutterstock.com:** arek_malang 80, AVAVA 78/(b) A, Cara-Foto 78/(a) A, connel 67/(a) D, CREATISTA 37tr, 37bl, dotshock 10t, EpicStockMedia 33r, goodluz 37tl, holbox 45tr, Jeanne Provost 18c, Karkas 109/C, Macrovector 18r, michaeljung 24tl, Olga Popova 109/A, Sean Lema 45tl, Tamara Kulikova 118, Val Thoermer 45br, Zoia Kostina 10c; **Sozaijiten:** 45tc

All other images © Pearson Education

Websites
Pearson Education Limited is not responsible for the content of any external internet sites. It is essential for tutors to preview each website before using it in class so as to ensure that the URL is still accurate, relevant and appropriate. We suggest that tutors bookmark useful websites and consider enabling students to access them through the school/college intranet.

Note from the publisher
Pearson has robust editorial processes, including answer and fact checks, to ensure the accuracy of the content in this publication, and every effort is made to ensure this publication is free of errors. We are, however, only human, and occasionally errors do occur. Pearson is not liable for any misunderstandings that arise as a result of errors in this publication, but it is our priority to ensure that the content is accurate. If you spot an error, please do contact us at resourcescorrections@pearson.com so we can make sure it is corrected.